GHOST STORIES
of
HOLLYWOOD

BARBARA SMITH

Illustrations by Arlana Anderson-Hale

LONE
PINE

Lone Pine Pu

D0181909

The Publisher: Lone Pine Publishing

10145 - 81 Avenue   1901 Raymond Ave. SW, Suite C
Edmonton, AB T6E 1W9   Renton, WA 98055
Canada   USA

Website: www.lonepinepublishing.com

Canadian Cataloguing in Publication Data
Smith, Barbara, 1947 –
   Ghost stories of Hollywood

   ISBN 1-55105-241-5

   1. Ghosts—California—Hollywood. 2. Legends—California—Hollywood.
I. Title.
GR580.S643 2000   398.2'09794'9405   C00-910795-9

Editorial Director: Nancy Foulds
Project Editor: Randy Williams
Production Manager: Jody Reekie
Book Design: Heather Markham, Arlana Anderson-Hale
Layout & Production: Arlana Anderson-Hale
Illustrations: Arlana Anderson-Hale
Photos Courtesy of: Barbara Smith

The stories, folklore and legends in this book are based on the author's collection of sources including individuals whose experiences have led them to
believe they have encountered phenomena of some kind or another. They are
meant to entertain, and neither the publisher nor the author claim these
stories represent fact.

We acknowledge the financial support of the Government of Canada through
the Book Publishing Industry Development Program (BPIDP) for our publishing activities.

PC: P6

Dedication

This book is lovingly dedicated to my grandsons, who—in keeping with Hollywood tradition—are listed in alphabetical order: Gregory and Joseph Trumbley.

For my grandsons and their peers—who will need forests as much as books—arrangements have been made to plant trees to compensate for the paper used in printing this volume.

Contents

Act 4: Ghosts in Public

Act 5: Ghostly Graveyards

Act 6: Stage Fright

Acknowledgments

It would not be possible for me to write any of my books without help. For this reason I owe a debt of thanks to many people. First of all, thank you to the talented paranormal investigators who have gone before. These people, who are often local experts, have done an invaluable job of researching possible explanations for particular hauntings. As a storyteller and folklore collector, my experience has been significantly enriched by their groundbreaking efforts.

Many people who have helped me with this volume have asked to remain anonymous. I have, of course, respected that request—but I do thank you one and all. Hollywood's Comedy Store, a building that once housed Ciro's Night Club and has been profiled in numerous articles and television specials as home to some very interesting paranormal specimens, unfortunately denied permission to use their story in this book. The employees openly admit that the club is haunted; however, it is also privately owned, and I have therefore accepted the owner's unexplained request.

My sincere thanks go to Marianne Boos, Sales Executive at the Hollywood Roosevelt Hotel, and the rest of the staff at that wonderful establishment, not only for their hospitality but also for the friendly support that went above and beyond the call of duty. Duncan St. James, owner and operator of TourLand USA, not only delighted me with two very full and exciting tours but then took the time to identify and return photographs that I sent to him. Thank you, Duncan.

The staff at Bonnie Doon Flowers in Edmonton identified the flowers in the bouquet at Marilyn Monroe's grave. My friend and fellow ghost story writer, Jo-Anne Christensen, shared not only her extensive resources but, perhaps more importantly, her contagious enthusiasm. Sociologist, author and dear friend Dr. Barrie Robinson generously and patiently contributed many creative ideas to the text of this book in addition to poring over every word of the manuscript while it was a work-in-progress. Thank you, Barrie—I hope you know how very much I value and appreciate your influence on my work. Thanks are also owed to my husband, Bob Smith, whose invaluable contribution to all of my books usually takes the form of a great many very thankless chores. Daena Smoller of the International Society for Psychical Research graciously shared her vast knowledge of the Vogue Theatre, which, in addition to being a highlight of this book, will also be featured in my upcoming book, *Stage Fright: Ghost Stories of the Theatre*, a work-in-progress that I look forward to completing very soon.

My efforts, and those of the people named above, would have been in vain without the amazing support I receive from the talented, generous and friendly people who make up the staff at Lone Pine Publishing. Unlike most authors I know, I have only ever had the kindest of comments to make about "my" publisher. I hope everyone at Lone Pine realizes how very much I value their efforts on my behalf. At this time I would like to single out two people for special thanks: Nancy Foulds and Randy Williams.

Introduction

The first dilemma I usually face when writing one of the books in the *Ghost Stories* series is to define exactly what I mean by the term "ghost." Anyone who has read one or more of my previous collections can attest to the fact that distilling the enormous number of often-contradictory indicators contained in the stories makes arriving at an acceptable definition difficult to say the least. But, before facing that dilemma, I had to confront an even bigger one.

I knew this book would present more challenges than the others. For instance, both *Ghost Stories of California* and *Ghost Stories of Washington* had easily defined geographic boundaries. Hollywood, however, is not so much a geographic area as it is a state of mind—a phenomenon that is a world unto itself or, at the very least, an entirely separate, larger-than-life culture within the realm of our everyday world. For this reason, and many others, Hollywood is a very special place.

Fortunately for our purposes here, one of the special qualities of "Tinseltown" is that it is a densely *haunted* place. I've found no other area the size of Hollywood with such an enormous volume of ghostly legacies entwined in its heritage.

I've heard it said that Hollywood is so thoroughly haunted because huge numbers of people have experienced negative emotions here. This theory is, at best, probably only partially true, because it is not just negative emotion that scars a psychic landscape and leaves a place haunted. In truth, any strong emotion can have that effect. People have also experienced great delight, success and ecstatic satisfaction as a result of being in and associated with Hollywood; those memory traces are also found in its ghostly echoes.

One legend states that the hauntings form a pattern flowing down and spreading out from the famous Hollywood sign that is so carefully arranged on the rugged terrain of Mount Lee in the Hollywood Hills. This is a delightfully romantic idea, but not one that holds up to examination. The Hollywood ghost stories that I've found simply don't follow any such pattern—they are as diverse in geography as they are in content and era.

The community of Hollywood is also haunted in a unique manner. In many ways, the people who became legends of the film industry's past continue to roam the streets of Hollywood today. As a result, a somewhat uneasy truce exists between the living and the dead. Some hauntings can be supernatural, such as when the ghost of a long-deceased movie star continues to reside in his or her old house. Other lingering presences are more mundane; the fact that old films have been preserved and still remain in circulation means that the pioneers of the film industry continue, in a sense, to haunt the souls of those living and acting today.

Movies have been filmed in and around Hollywood for more than 85 years now. By the time the 1970s and '80s rolled around, the area had become badly deteriorated and was, in fact, one of the seediest parts of L.A. As a component of a very successful campaign to make Hollywood a more appealing place, a great deal of effort has gone into urban renewal and rejuvenation. That process has seen the installation of a series of signs along Hollywood Boulevard denoting historic points of interest along a self-guided

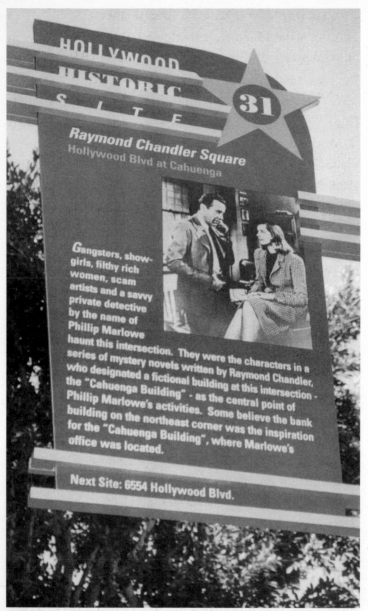

The historic site marker at this intersection on Hollywood Boulevard states that the area is "haunted" by fictional characters. It is also haunted by very real ghosts.

walking tour. Site number 31, located at the intersection of Hollywood and Cahuenga Boulevards, has been designated "Raymond Chandler Square" as a tribute to the creator of the enduring private eye character Phillip Marlowe, star of a series of hardboiled detective novels including *The Big Sleep*, *The Long Goodbye* and *Farewell, My Lovely* (and their inevitable film adaptations, in which Marlowe has been played by everyone from legends such as Humphrey Bogart, Dick Powell and Robert Mitchum to more contemporary actors such as James Garner and Elliot Gould). Chandler placed the action in many episodes of his popular Marlowe series at that very intersection. The explanatory text on the sign reads, in part, "Gangsters, showgirls, filthy rich women, scam artists and a savvy private detective by the name of Phillip Marlowe *haunt* this intersection" (emphasis mine). While the past should never be forgotten in any field of endeavor, the unique nature of the film industry ensures that it is all but impossible not to remember or to be haunted by its founders.

Because Hollywood is much more than just a geographical location within the city of Los Angeles, I have chosen to include in this book any ghostly anecdotes which relate to the motion picture industry. Admittedly, some of my choices are arbitrary and you may wish to argue for or against inclusion of a particular story. As hard as it may be to believe, Hollywood was conceived of and intended as "a model of Christian virtue" in the last days of the 19th century; it rather rapidly became a hive of selfish and often immoral activity when the motion picture business settled in, so controversy and disagreement over the area's history is hardly new.

These controversies may have been a legitimate part of Hollywood's history, but I wanted to write this book with as little conflict as possible. Toward that end, I booked myself a flight to L.A., a room in the haunted Hollywood Roosevelt Hotel, and a place on the tours offered by TourLand USA. Right from the beginning, nothing about this research trip was ordinary.

Although I've stayed in many hotel rooms, I've rarely felt as immediately comfortable as I did in my eighth floor suite at the Roosevelt. As soon as I was unpacked and settled in, I made my way up to the floor directly above me—the very haunted ninth floor. As I was taking pictures of the hallway and the door to room 928, which the ghost of Montgomery Clift is thought to haunt, I had to smile at the sign on the door indicating that it was now designated a "no smoking" area. Because Clift was in life a heavy smoker, he would not have been comfortable with *that* little restriction. Even though I didn't feel his spirit anywhere in the corridor, I did say "hello" to the long-deceased actor on the off-chance that his presence might have been aware of *mine*. Montgomery Clift was an actor whose work I greatly admired, and I would have hated to miss an opportunity to pay my sincere respects.

That evening, a Saturday, I took a cab to the Beverly Center, where I was to meet some fellow tourists and our tour guide, Duncan St. James, owner and operator of TourLand USA. Together we were about to embark on a drive around haunted Hollywood in a 1971 Cadillac hearse. What better way to conduct the research necessary to write this book?

The sights, sounds and abundance of eerie information that the tour provided had me frantically taking

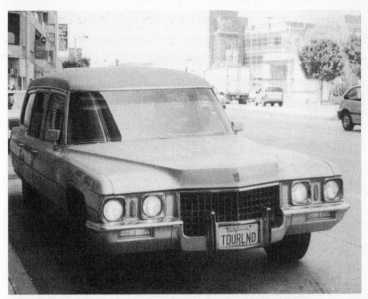

This 1971 Cadillac hearse, operated by TourLand USA, is an appropriate vehicle from which to track the ghosts of Hollywood.

notes throughout my first drive around the area. Several hours later, virtually overwhelmed by information, I said good-bye to Duncan—who reminded me to meet him again on Monday afternoon, when he would be offering a different tour.

I retired to my room and tried to transcribe the scrawl of notes I'd taken before I forgot any details of the exciting, exhausting day I'd just had. That attended to, I decided to read in bed before turning in for the night. Some minutes later I realized that I was not reading at all. In fact, the book had fallen to my lap and I was lost in thought, concentrating on the task I had ahead of me in compiling and writing *Ghost Stories of Hollywood*.

In order to complete the other books in this series, I have done quite a bit of investigation into the lives of people involved in the early days of Hollywood. In the course of that research I'd developed a great deal of respect for those film industry pioneers. It was extremely important to me that I handle their stories with respect and skill. Rather than reading the novel I'd brought with me as entertainment, I found I was pondering how best to tell their ghost stories. With that, the bedside lamp, which had been the only light on in the room, went dark. It did not turn off. The switch remained in the "on" position. The bulb did not burn out. The light emanating from that bulb in that lamp simply ceased to shine. I sat still in the dark for at least a minute before the light bulb just as mysteriously began to again shine as it should. I was not unnerved by this strange incident, but somehow comforted. It seemed to me that some force beyond my control wanted to make itself known to me, to assure me that my efforts at remembering those involved in the movie industry's infancy would be satisfactory. So assured, I turned off the light and slept through the night.

Two days later, right on schedule at 1:00 in the afternoon, the now-familiar hearse pulled up to the same meeting place. While the six other tourists settled themselves into the vehicle, Duncan and I greeted each other like old friends. I was eager to be transported to even more locations in and around Hollywood where stars had died or their ghosts had been seen. The afternoon was magical. Although we didn't see any ghosts, we certainly paid tribute to some very accomplished people. We also experienced an incident that made us wonder if at least one ghost might have tagged along for the fun.

Part of the running commentary that Duncan supplies while he is escorting these tours is done live—improv style,

The author with Duncan St. James, owner and operator of TourLand USA, an enterprise that specializes in ghost tours!

if you will. Other portions he has recorded on audio tapes that he cues up and plays at appropriate moments. Shortly after we left Westwood Memorial Park—where, among other graves, we visited Marilyn Monroe's crypt—the tape player in the hearse came on of its own volition. For just a few bars, we passengers were all entranced to hear Elton John's "Candle in the Wind"—a musical tribute to Marilyn Monroe! Duncan, however, didn't have the luxury of that giddy feeling because he knew that what had just happened was physically impossible. "That song isn't even on that part of the track," he muttered in obvious confusion. Presumably Marilyn Monroe, one of the most active ghosts in Hollywood, had just wanted us to know that she'd been with us the only way she could be—as a ghost.

After some nervous comments from all of us, we fell quiet for a moment. I don't know about the rest of those in the hearse, but I for one was wondering just what had happened. Did a ghost really join us? And if so, would I ever really be able to find a satisfyingly accurate definition for what a ghost is?

Over the past 10 years I have devoted considerable effort to formalizing just such a definition so that I can have some confidence that my readers and I share a perspective. Unfortunately, I'm no closer to my goal now that when I started. This conundrum extends to several related—and possibly unanswerable—questions. Why are ghosts here? Why are some people so much more likely than others to see a ghost? Why are some locations haunted while other places, where equally traumatic events have occurred, remain "cold" (that is, uninhabited by spirits)?

Although my investigations have not supplied me with the concise definition I've been after, they have definitely taught me what a ghost is *not*. A ghost is not a cute, white cartoon character, nor a human figure draped in a sheet. A ghost is also not, necessarily, a filmy, gauzy apparition—although some certainly do fit that description. Ghosts do not exist to scare us. I believe that most of these otherworldly presences are simply unaware—or unwilling to accept—that they are no longer living. Other ghosts, however, seem to haunt for a particular reason. The ghost of "Bugsy" Siegel (p. 68) is an excellent example of such a haunting. The sudden shock of the death of Siegel's physical body caused the energy of his spirit to remain in the spot where the trauma had occurred.

Not all ghosts present themselves visually in the shape of humans. Those that do are more properly called apparitions. Just because a ghost is not seen (i.e., is not an apparition) does not mean that there isn't a spirit in the vicinity. The specter may manifest itself only in the form of a sensation—that feeling that you are not alone even though no one else is physically present. Ghosts can also manifest as odors—both pleasant and unpleasant. Other evidence of a paranormal occurrence can include ghostly lights and even phantom music.

A "poltergeist" is a rare type of spectral being that can be identified by its noisy and even violent behavior. This type of ghost will often move objects with great force and can wreak considerable havoc on its surrounding environment. Poltergeists are associated with individuals rather than with places. They have been known to follow people for years, even through a succession of moves from one residence to another.

Retrocognition, which has been described as seeing or in some other manner *sensing* the past, is an especially fascinating type of ghostly phenomenon. Some students of the paranormal believe that most, if not all, hauntings can be attributed to retrocognition. Retrocognition is defined as a temporary displacement in time; this dislocation allows the person affected an opportunity to review or experience historical events. In other words, the energy once created is somehow detected and replayed in a manner that can be likened to either an audio- or videotape on a continuous loop. The psychic energy exuded has become anchored in the atmosphere. Acceptance of this theory implies a "place memory"—the concept that certain events are embedded in a given place and continue to resonate. These are also called "residual hauntings."

It has been suggested that retrocognition (also known as postcognition) actually occurs much more frequently than is commonly recognized, but that the fleeting temporal displacement is simply written off as the witness's imagination. If this is so, then perhaps we should be paying closer attention to momentary shifts in our perception when we experience them. The Hollywood-based stories of The Pines (p. 154) provides a classic example of this fascinating concept.

The opposite of retrocognition is precognition—seeing or sensing an event that has not yet occurred. When such an experience is accompanied by a presence or ghost, the presence is called a "forerunner."

One further type of phantom energy is the manifestation of ghost lights or ignes fatui. These luminous paranormal occurrences, which often occur in cemeteries, have fascinated countless people over the centuries.

But why do spectral phenomena exist? The theory of "leftover energy"—physical and emotional—is frequently used to explain the existence of ghosts. This theory is closely related to the concept of "psychic imprint"—the idea that the essence of a person or an event has somehow been "stamped" onto the environment in which that person lived or a traumatic or violent event took place. The deceased person's soul has effectively left an indelible mark on the physical world; in simple terms, he or she has become a ghost.

Because some people are so much more likely than others to be aware of a ghost's presence, it is possible that spirits are all around us but are detectable only by our (nearly atrophied) sixth sense. Rather than perceiving otherworldly sensations with our familiar five senses, we may only notice the hair on our arms or on the back of our necks standing on end, or become aware of a generalized tingling sensation in our skin. And what of that disconcerting feeling that we are not alone—that we are being watched, even though our five senses fail to confirm the existence of any other presence nearby? Scientists have suggested that humans do indeed possess a rarely used sixth sense, located in the vomeronasal organ (in the nose), that is capable of detecting pheromones—chemicals released into the air in minute quantities by many species as a way of communicating with others of their kind.

Perhaps the vomeronasal organ also detects or senses energies exuded from disembodied spirits but, because we are not used to consciously responding to messages from this sense, we are unable to recognize the messages as anything more than a vague feeling that "something" is close to us. It is quite possible that some humans are more sensitive to such subtleties than others. Children, for example, seem to be more sensitive to otherworldly presences than adults. Over time most adults have come to rely almost exclusively on their other five senses and therefore ignore—or fail to respond to—sensations picked up by their sixth sense.

Those adults who *do* seem to recognize and act upon messages from their sixth sense are usually referred to as "psychics" or "sensitives." Though this sensitivity is likely inborn, it can apparently be enhanced with practice—or diminished through neglect. Perhaps the variations in sensitivity from person to person explain why some people are more likely than others to encounter a ghost.

Behind all of these suppositions lurks a further unknown: Does a ghostly encounter originate with the living person who is experiencing the encounter, or with the ghost itself? The answer is debatable but, because many people have reported seeing or sensing the same spirit either at the same or different times, the entities and events chronicled in this book are unlikely to be mere figments of the observers' imaginations.

Being haunted is not necessarily a permanent status for either a person or a place. A location that is currently haunted may not always be so. Conversely, just because your home and workplace are now ghost-free zones, there is no guarantee that they will remain in that condition indefinitely.

Some forms of this ghostly energy are incredibly tenacious. For example, the ghosts of Roman soldiers are still occasionally spotted roaming the English countryside where they battled centuries ago, but few ghosts are that ancient. Because I've never heard or read of any place or person being haunted by the ghost of a prehistoric cave dweller, I presume that, like all forms of energy, ghosts eventually weaken and dissipate.

In the presence of a ghost or during an active haunting, witnesses will usually note predictable and distinguishable changes in their environment. Such changes often include a sudden, dramatic temperature drop that is localized, though it may encompass a large area. Drafts, odors or noises—all of which are apparently sourceless—may also be present.

Despite a lack of agreement on what a ghost might be, or from whence they come, the phenomena exist in all cultures and have been noted throughout history. Rather than becoming philosophical about the nature of different sorts of hauntings and ghosts, perhaps we would best be served by attempting to accept them as a part of our world—a part that we don't, as yet, fully understand, but one that exists nonetheless. Only a few hundred years ago, lightning was considered to be a preternatural or paranormal occurrence. Our current knowledge of ghosts may be today's parallel to that situation.

My personal experience collecting ghost stories has taught me to accept one particular consistency: A paranormal encounter is a profoundly moving event. I have yet to have a story told to me in a flippant or even matter-of-fact manner. Out of respect for this emotional factor, I have always agreed to protect a contributor's anonymity whenever he or she has requested that I do so.

The narratives in this book are reports of real events. We all know that life, as we live it, is anything but neat. As a result, these accounts tend to be a bit more ragged than the stories we are used to reading. A fictional tale of a haunting will be structured with a predictable presentation: a beginning, a middle and an end. The incidents recorded here refuse to be that orderly. Sometimes they are merely fragments, which can be somewhat frustrating in a world so fond of tidy resolutions. We tend to find it more satisfying when loose ends are bound up in the last sentence of a tale. Nonetheless, I hope you will find—as I have come to—that in the instances where there isn't enough information to tell a traditional story, the parts that are missing are every bit as provocative as the parts that remain.

This collection is not intended as an attempt to alter anyone's belief system with my personal convictions or explanations. My intent is to entertain and to possibly prompt thought in areas that you might not otherwise have considered exploring. Though I do not pretend to be an educator, if reading this book introduces you to facets of the film industry or Hollywood's history with which you were previously unfamiliar, then I will be delighted.

If you have any ghost stories or personal experiences with the paranormal that you would like to share, please contact me through Lone Pine Publishing. I'd love to hear from you. In the meantime, do enjoy this unique hooray for Hollywood!

Act **1**

HOLLYWOOD

Haunted Houses

Playbill

George Reeves (1914–1959)

Gone with the Wind (1939)

The Adventures of Superman
(TV series, 1953–1957)

Clifton Webb (1889–1966)

Laura (1944)

The Razor's Edge (1946)

Mr. Belvedere Goes to College (1949)

Cheaper by the Dozen (1950)

Stars and Stripes Forever (1952)

Titanic (1953)

Three Coins in the Fountain (1954)

Mary Pickford (1892–1979)

The Poor Little Rich Girl (1917)

Rebecca of Sunnybrook Farm (1917)

Daddy Long Legs (1919)

Pollyanna (1920)

Little Lord Fauntleroy (1921)

My Best Girl (1927)

Coquette (1929)

The Taming of the Shrew (1929)

Douglas Fairbanks (1883–1939)

The Mask of Zorro (1920)

The Three Musketeers (1921)

Robin Hood (1922)

The Thief of Bagdad (1924)

Don Q, Son of Zorro (1925)

The Black Pirate (1926)

The Iron Mask (1929)

The Taming of the Shrew (1929)

Mr. Robinson Crusoe (1932)

The Private Life of Don Juan (1934)

William S. Hart (1864–1946)

His Hour of Manhood (1914)

In the Sage Brush Country (1914)

The Man From Nowhere (1915)

Hell's Hinges (1916)

O'Malley of the Mounted (1921)

Wild Bill Hickok (1923)

Tumbleweeds (1925)

Harry Houdini (1874–1926)

The Grim Game (1919)

Terror Island (1919)

The Man from Beyond (1922)

Rudolph Valentino (1895–1926)

The Four Horsemen of the Apocalypse (1921)

The Sheik (1921)

Blood and Sand (1922)

Monsieur Beaucaire (1924)

The Eagle (1925)

Son of the Sheik (1926)

Benjamin "Bugsy" Siegel (1906–1947)

Occupation: Gangster

Lionel Barrymore (1878–1954)

West of Zanzibar (1928)

Mata Hari (1931)

Grand Hotel (1932)

Dinner at Eight (1933)

Treasure Island (1934)

David Copperfield (1935)

Captains Courageous (1937)

Young Dr. Kildare (1938)

It's a Wonderful Life (1946)

Duel in the Sun (1946)

Key Largo (1948)

Ethel Barrymore (1879–1959)

The Final Judgment (1915)

Rasputin and the Empress (1932)

None But the Lonely Heart (1944)

The Farmer's Daughter (1947)

The Paradine Case (1947)

Deadline USA (1952)

Young At Heart (1955)

John Barrymore (1882–1942)

Dr. Jekyll and Mr. Hyde (1920)

Sherlock Holmes (1922)

Beau Brummel (1924)

Don Juan (1926)

Moby Dick (1930)

Rasputin and the Empress (1932)

Grand Hotel (1932)

Dinner At Eight (1933)

Twentieth Century (1934)

Bulldog Drummond's Revenge (1937)

Jayne Mansfield (1933-1967)

The Girl Can't Help It (1956)

Female Jungle
(AKA *The Hangover*) (1956)

*Will Success Spoil
Rock Hunter?* (1957)

Kiss Them for Me (1957)

Too Hot to Handle (1959)

Hercules and the Hydra
(AKA *The Loves of Hercules*) (1960)

Promises, Promises (1963)

The Las Vegas Hillbillys (1966)

Single Room Furnished (1968)

Jean Harlow (1911-1937)

Hell's Angels (1930)

The Public Enemy (1931)

Red-Headed Woman (1932)

Red Dust (1932)

Hold Your Man (1933)

Dinner at Eight (1933)

Bombshell (1933)

China Seas (1935)

Libeled Lady (1936)

Saratoga (1937)

Thelma Todd (1906-1935)

The Haunted House (1928)

Abie's Irish Rose (1929)

The House of Horror (1929)

The Bachelor Girl (1929)

The Pajama Party (1931)

Monkey Business (1931)

Horse Feathers (1932)

The Devil's Brother (1933)

Hips, Hips, Hooray (1934)

Palooka (1934)

The Bohemian Girl (1936)

Lucille Ball (1911-1989)

Roberta (1934)

Stage Door (1937)

Room Service (1938)

You Can't Fool Your Wife (1940)

Sorrowful Jones (1949)

The Fuller Brush Girl (1950)

Fancy Pants (1950)

I Love Lucy (TV series, 1951-1957)

The Long, Long Trailer (1954)

The Lucy-Desi Comedy Hour (TV series, 1957-1960)

The Lucy Show (TV series, 1962-1968)

Here's Lucy (TV series, 1968-1974)

Mame (1974)

Life with Lucy (TV series, 1986)

Ozzie Nelson (1906-1975)

Take It Big (1944)

People Are Funny (1946)

The Adventures of Ozzie and Harriet (TV series, 1952–1966)

Harriet Nelson (1909-1994)

Follow the Fleet (1936)

Take It Big (1944)

The Adventures of Ozzie and Harriet
(TV series, 1952–1966)

David Nelson (1936-)

The Adventures of Ozzie and Harriet
(TV series, 1952–1966)

Peyton Place (1957)

Ricky Nelson (1940-1985)

The Adventures of Ozzie and Harriet
(TV series, 1952–1966)

Rio Bravo (1959)

The Wackiest Ship in the Army (1960)

Robert Taylor (1911-1969)

Broadway Melody of 1938 (1937)

A Yank at Oxford (1938)

Billy the Kid (1941)

Bataan (1943)

Quo Vadis? (1951)

Ivanhoe (1952)

Knights of the Round Table (1953)

D-Day: The Sixth of June (1956)

Miracle of the White Stallions (1963)

Glamorous Ghosts

Some of the most beautiful women ever, anywhere in the world, have been associated with Hollywood. Sadly, some of those same glamorous Hollywood stars have led heartbreakingly tragic lives—right up to the moment of their deaths. Perhaps that is why the spirits of Jean Harlow, Jayne Mansfield, Marilyn Monroe (whose ghost story is described in The Spirit's Inn chapter, beginning on p. 86) and Thelma Todd have continued to haunt our earthly plane long after their deaths. The following chronicles explore some aspects of the lives, deaths and afterlives of these talented and gorgeous women.

* * *

In 1926, 20-year-old Thelma Todd debuted as a movie actress. Her extraordinary beauty translated onto the screen so well that she was soon being called "The Blonde Venus," "The Ice Cream Blonde" and "The Hot Toddy." During the next nine years, Todd made more than 100 movies, proving herself to be a talented and hard-working actress.

Todd was also a very practical and sensible woman. She realized that her movie career, like all others, had the potential to end as quickly as it had begun. In order to protect herself from financial devastation in that eventuality, the actress opened a restaurant called Thelma Todd's Sidewalk Café. In managing and developing that endeavor, she demonstrated impressive business acumen.

None of those admirable attributes could prevent her

tragic and untimely death. Some time in the earliest hours of December 16, 1935, the actress's thriving career—and her life—came to a sudden and premature end.

When her maid found Thelma's crumpled form behind the wheel of her car in the garage, the servant initially thought that the star had over-indulged at one of the parties she loved so much. The maid's reaction was certainly reasonable. After all, the beautiful Todd was still wearing her party-going clothes and accessories—an evening gown, a full-length mink coat and $20,000 worth of jewelry.

After a second assessment, however, the maid realized that her employer was not merely passed out; Thelma Todd was dead. Racing from the garage to the house, the distraught servant phoned the police. The authorities' more detailed check of the body determined that the gorgeous woman, her car, and even the garage floor under the vehicle were all splattered with blood. After examining the area, the police transported Todd's body to the medical examiner's office. Despite ample evidence to the contrary, the coroner officially determined that the movie star's death was an accidental suicide caused by carbon monoxide poisoning.

Not surprisingly, Thelma Todd's next-of-kin disagreed with this determination. Her mother, Alice Todd, fought to have the death investigated further. Alice was aware that, like herself, Thelma had a bad habit of associating with men who could be called disreputable at best. The young actress had been married only once, and then for just a couple of years. The night before her death, Thelma's ex-husband, Pasquale DiCicco, an unsavory character with known underworld connections, had been at the same party as she, and the two were seen arguing explosively.

Lucky Luciano, generally considered the most dangerous mobster in America at that time, was a friend of DiCicco's. It was known that the dreaded gangster had made a veiled threat against Todd's life after she had refused to cooperate with a proposed business undertaking. Most people who knew Todd agreed that this situation had lethal possibilities.

With all of these potentially deadly circumstances swirling around her, Thelma left the party. Her chauffeur for the evening later reported that a car had been following theirs all the way to Todd's home and that the actress had said that she was afraid of the mob. From that point on, exactly how the night's events unfolded is confusing at best and occasionally even contradictory. Thelma's live-in lover, Roland West, a movie director who specialized in films with complex murder plots, admitted to authorities that he had pushed Todd out of the house and refused to let her back in following a heated argument that was overheard by several witnesses. An autopsy revealed that the deceased had eaten food that had not been served at the party she attended just prior to her death, but where, when and with whom she dined is unknown.

Given these horrific and convoluted circumstances, to say nothing of the condition in which Thelma Todd's body was found, Alice Todd's protestations against the official ruling of suicide made a great deal of sense. The fact that the older woman suddenly and inexplicably stopped pursuing the case perhaps lends credence to the theory that Thelma Todd was murdered by members of a vicious and powerful underworld.

Despite what seemed like convincing proof to the contrary, Todd's death was officially recorded as having been "accidentally caused." No charges were ever laid in connection with her death; someone, or perhaps several people cooperating with one another, probably got away with murder on that long-ago mid-December night.

This injustice is possibly what has caused Thelma Todd's spirit to be so restless. Her ghost is still frequently seen—and felt—in the building at 17575 Pacific Coast Highway where Todd's restaurant was located. Staff with the production company now located there have spoken of seeing a filmy apparition resembling the deceased screen idol. They say the ghost most often materializes at the top of a staircase before floating toward an outside courtyard area.

In the garage at 17531 Posetano Road where Todd died, people have complained of hearing the sounds of an engine running, and even of smelling noxious exhaust fumes when the area appears to be empty. As it is highly unlikely that justice will now ever be served, it seems reasonable to expect that Thelma Todd's active haunting will continue for some time to come.

* * *

There are many parallels between Thelma Todd and Jean Harlow. Like Todd, Harlow's exquisite beauty also earned her a nickname—"The Blonde Bombshell" being the moniker that so aptly described the platinum- haired actress. She was not only beautiful but also quite daring for her era. Harlow exuded a sensuality on the screen that, in the 1930s, was both exciting and novel. Like most actresses of her time, Harlow began her career with bit-part roles in

Glamorous actress Jean Harlow's star on Hollywood's Walk of Fame is chipped and in need of repair. Perhaps this is one of the reasons that Harlow's spirit has not rested in peace.

movies. However, after the wealthy and eccentric film producer Howard Hughes noticed her, Jean Harlow was immediately on the fast track to professional success.

Sadly, Harlow also had an unfortunate personality characteristic in common with Thelma Todd. She too had considerably less than discerning taste in men. Paul Bern, Jean Harlow's second husband, beat her severely and frequently. Those beatings eventually led directly to her untimely death.

Despite his violent treatment of her, Jean Harlow loved Bern so much that, when he killed himself, she was so distraught that she too attempted suicide. Even though her attempt was not successful, Harlow's days were numbered. Five years later, in 1937, the "Blonde Bombshell" succumbed at the age of 26 to kidney damage originally caused by Bern's savage beatings.

The first reported ghost sighting in the house she and Bern had shared was a grisly one, but it was not the ghost of Harlow who was seen—it was the image of Paul Bern. By that time, the house belonged to Jay Sebring, a popular Hollywood hair stylist. In 1966, while Sebring was away on business, his girlfriend, Sharon Tate, woke to find Bern's ghost stumbling around the bedroom in which she was sleeping.

Terrified, Tate fled downstairs where an even more upsetting vision awaited her—the image of a human form tied to the stair rail, bleeding from slashes to the throat and quite obviously dying. Now Tate was trapped—ghostly sounds echoed from the floor above her and dreadfully gruesome ghostly sights confronted her on the main floor. Perhaps because she felt responsible for watching over her boyfriend's house, Sharon Tate did not physically flee, but rather drowned her fear with vodka in order to pass out.

Upon Sebring's return, Tate told him about her horrifying visions of the night before. His reactions to her account of the incidents are not recorded, but history does tell us that in 1969 Sharon Tate was one of several people slaughtered by Charles Manson's "family." The victims' bodies were found bound, their throats slashed. Somehow the sight of Paul Bern's tortured spirit must have triggered for Tate a ghastly precognitive experience which foretold her own death in another house.

The woman who bought the house in the mid-1980s first became aware that there was something eerie about the place even before she and her family had moved in. She reported hearing a distinctly feminine voice whispering ghostly pleas for help. During the first night the family spent in the house, a strong but invisible force banged up against the bed where the woman and her husband lay. Since then, the couple has also heard phantom sounds of a woman sobbing on several occasions when all the members of the family were gathered together and none of them was crying. This anomaly was always accompanied by an oppressive feeling of melancholy.

With great justification, the family assumed that what they were hearing was simply a psychic replay of Harlow's overwhelming grief at the loss of her husband. Fortunately, not all the auditory enigmas in the house were sad ones. Distant sounds of a party have also been heard coming from inside a particular bedroom closet.

At other times the paranormal manifestations provided more standard indications that the house was haunted. Inexplicable cold spots and drafts would randomly materialize and remain for varying lengths of time. Footsteps would be heard shuffling through the house and moving up and down the stairs when there were no family members walking about. A distinct fragrance could sometimes be detected in one of the bedrooms where there was never any perfume or cologne.

The family had no way of knowing whether the ghost was that of Jean Harlow or her husband, Paul Bern, but one of the ghostly inhabitants of their house liked to attract attention to itself by knocking quietly on the front door and playing with a particular light switch in the kitchen.

When the house where Jean Harlow and Paul Bern once lived was again investigated for supernatural occurrences 20 years later, it was a considerably calmer place, with only Harlow's gentle spirit occasionally visiting from beyond the veil.

* * *

The linking parallels among these glamorous ghosts continues with the life and afterlife of Jayne Mansfield, who was a contemporary of Marilyn Monroe's. One of Mansfield's and Monroe's other acquaintances was Anton LaVey, the High Priest of the Church of Satan. In 1973, 11 years after Marilyn Monroe's death, LaVey successfully summoned her presence during a séance he was conducting.

That demonstration of supernatural power may have been impressive, but it was small potatoes if you subscribe to the widely held belief that LaVey killed Jayne Mansfield and her boyfriend with a deadly curse.

A curvy 40-22-35 when she won the title of "Miss Photoflash of 1952," Vera Jane Palmer changed her name to Jayne Mansfield and landed a series of film appearances in the '50s and early '60s, usually playing stereotypical "dumb blonde" roles. Mansfield was initially cast in respectable productions, but by the mid-'60s these roles had almost completely dried up and she was appearing in awful Italian-made sex comedies and sub-mainstream drive-in fodder.

By 1966, Mansfield was in a serious downward spiral. Her movie career was all but over, and she had begun touring in a burlesque show to cover her staggering tax debts. Even worse, her personal life was in a shambles. After three failed marriages, Mansfield had fallen in with a high-profile but unscrupulous Hollywood lawyer named Sam Brody.

Mansfield originally hired Brody to represent her in the divorce from husband number three, but the actress and the lawyer were soon an item. Their relationship was a stormy one into which overindulgence in alcohol and physical abuse were commonly introduced.

The degree to which Mansfield and Brody were involved with the Church of Satan seems to depend on which account of the situation one examines. Some researchers indicate that the beautiful actress was a practicing member of the group and that Brody was appalled by her involvement. Those close to Mansfield's family have maintained that the actress had no ties to the Church whatsoever apart from some photos that she and LaVey had taken together as a publicity stunt. According to this version of events, LaVey was smitten with the curvaceous entertainer but was repeatedly teased and spurned by her. Many believe that LaVey later spread lies about his involvement with Mansfield—and her involvement with his church—as a means of attracting further notoriety. Numerous published reports *do* imply that both Mansfield and Brody were attending services at the Church of Satan, but we may never know if these stories are merely urban legends brought about by LaVey's incessant self-promotion.

What is commonly accepted is that Brody and LaVey despised one another. The men's feelings were known to be intense enough that many think LaVey laid a death curse on both Jayne Mansfield and Sam Brody. If that rumor is true, then the curse was a successful one.

On the night of June 29, 1967, Sam Brody, Jayne Mansfield and Mansfield's three children left a club gig in Biloxi, Mississippi on a drive to New Orleans in a chauffeur-driven Buick. Many miles away in Dallas, Vera Peers, Jayne Mansfield's mother, was awakened at that very moment from a sound sleep. She was certain that her daughter had been calling out to her, begging for help. It took the older woman several minutes to shake off the effects of what she thought was a disturbing dream. Eventually, however, Peers was able to fall back to sleep. As soon as she lost consciousness, Jayne came to her again, smiling peacefully and urging her mother to be cautious but not afraid.

Moments later, the woman awoke with a start again, this time to the sound of someone pounding on her door. It was the local police. They had come to inform the movie star's mother that her daughter and grandchildren had been involved in a car accident.

While en route to New Orleans, the car in which Mansfield had been riding was suddenly engulfed in a thick cloud of mosquito pesticide. This made it impossible for the driver to see the 18-wheeler that had slowed ahead of them, and their vehicle plowed under its trailer at full speed. The force of the collision sheared the roof off the Buick. The children, who'd been asleep in the back seat, were not seriously injured, but the adults—who had been in the front seat—were all killed on impact. Contrary to a popular and persistent rumor, police photos taken at the accident scene clearly show that the actress was not decapitated in the collision—she was scalped.

Hauntings began almost immediately, with Jayne's spirit manifesting at her own funeral. The ritual was held in a chapel that was lit by amber-colored light bulbs. During the service, those lights suddenly and inexplicably flared to the brightness of floodlights. That intensity held for some 30 seconds while the bulb above the altar exuded an odd, heart-shaped aura. The strange sight convinced those gathered that Jayne's spirit was with them, because heart-shaped objects and the color pink were both part of Jayne's signature look.

Once the glare subsided, the ceremony continued as planned. The fixtures were later checked thoroughly. The filaments in the bulbs, which should have been burned out by the increased voltage, proved to be unaffected by the anomaly. Impossibly, no damage had been done to any of them. Even LaVey conceded, "I think Jayne wanted to let us know that she is still with us."

If his presumption is correct, then Jayne Mansfield's spirit continued to want acknowledgment; many years after her death, her ghost was frequently seen at her former mansion in the Hollywood Hills. Most often, the readily recognizable apparition was seen lounging beside the heart-shaped swimming pool.

According to the children's nanny, the deceased woman frequently came back to talk to her children. The servant reported that she had observed the children in conversation with someone or something that she could not see. After these chats, the youngsters would explain, in a matter-of-fact manner, that their mother had come to visit them.

But even then the power of LaVey's curse had not expired. Over the next few years, many people connected with either Jayne or her palatial home had to deal with considerably more than just ghost sightings. The number of tragedies associated with Mansfield's house certainly supported the theory that an effective curse had been laid upon the deceased woman.

During the clean-up and repair process necessary after water pipes in "The Pink Palace" burst for no apparent reason, workers reported watching objects moving around rooms on their own volition. Many said that they felt they were not alone, even though their five familiar senses assured them that they were. A plumber was badly frightened when he felt himself being touched by an invisible hand. To add to his concern, seconds later he heard what seemed to be the sounds of distant moaning. Several workers refused to re-enter the house after having what they would only describe as "an unexplainable experience" on that job site.

Over the next 11 years, the house had no fewer than five different occupants, all of whom suffered tragedies during their residency. The first family lost their teenage son after he was killed in an accident, joy-riding in a pink car he had found on the property. It had been a gift from one of Jayne's many admirers.

Cass Elliot, a member of the singing group The Mamas and The Papas, moved into the house next. Shortly after she'd settled into her new home, Elliot went to England on business. While there, she choked to death on a sandwich.

The anomaly in Mansfield's former home that was easiest to tie to Jayne was a female occupant's sudden obsession with dying her hair platinum blonde and having her breast size enhanced. When the woman found a trunk full of the dead movie star's clothes, she began to wear them. Her friends soon confronted her about the bizarre behavior they were noticing. She said she had no idea why her personality and style were changing so radically—they just were. The woman's transformation continued until she heard a disembodied female voice ordering her to "get out." She did, and she never returned.

When former Beatle Ringo Starr bought the house, the first thing he did was to apply white paint to cover Jayne Mansfield's choice of pink on the exterior walls. His attempt at redecorating was only successful for a short time. Before long, the house began reverting to pink, the color Jayne Mansfield loved above any other.

Skeptics might blame that oddity on the use of poor-quality paint or the fact that pink can be a difficult color to cover, especially with white paint. While acknowledging those possibilities, in light of all the other bizarre happenings associated with the house it seems equally possible that some supernatural force was at work here—especially considering that the next time a finish coat of white paint was applied, it was a double application on top of a coat of sealer. The person responsible for having the house redone to Starr's specification was at a loss when the house once again began to turn pink. Neither paint experts nor chemists were ever able to solve the perplexing problem, but whatever was causing the strange change in color must have weakened over time, because the house is now another color.

As if the house had not already been through enough upheaval, it was occupied next by a congregation from the Church of Satan. This meant that the people who were in and out of the house on a regular basis were Satanists—and therefore quite accustomed to the sensations conjured up by a supernatural presence. However, even they reported feeling a constant unwanted presence—that of Jayne Mansfield.

While all of these strange events were transpiring at the Pink Palace, a writer named May Mann was hard at work finishing off the final chapters of a book about Jayne Mansfield's life. Mann was anxious to have the project completed; as she worked on it, Mann reportedly heard Jayne's voice calling out, begging for help. The author was even more dismayed when she found most of her manuscript pages splattered with blood. No one had been near the sheets of paper since the author had put them away the night before—and the stains had certainly not been there at that time.

The next person to own the house had, ironically, once been in a romantic relationship with Mansfield. Singer Engelbert Humperdinck had heard rumors about the property being haunted, so he had the place exorcised before he moved in. He always maintained that the rite had been successful and that he never detected a specter of any kind in or around the house. One hopes that Jayne Mansfield has, by now, found the peace that eluded her for so much of her life—and her afterlife.

* * *

The numbers of similarities found in the stories of these glamorous women—and their ghosts—is remarkable enough for the "coincidences" alone to be considered something of a paranormal enigma.

Super Specter

On a fine summer evening, when he was only 10 years old, Jimmy Stein biked four miles from his home in Beverly Glen Park to the adventure of a lifetime. As was common with many children of his age, Jimmy was fascinated by Superman. This particular night was, in fact, the boy's second journey to his hero's home. When he'd made the trek the year before, Jim had timed his visit poorly. Even though he waited patiently for several hours, the legendary Last Son of Krypton—or more correctly, George Reeves, the actor who played the role of the superhero on the popular television show *The Adventures of Superman*—had not been at home.

On his second excursion, the little boy held out no real hope of actually seeing the Man of Steel. He only wanted to peer inside his hero's house. As he pedaled toward the secluded residence at 1579 Benedict Canyon Drive, Jimmy was somewhat unnerved to see that he was not the first to arrive. There, sitting in a cruiser in front of the house Jimmy knew as Superman's, were a pair of real-life authority figures—police officers.

Hoping to avoid being seen, Jimmy laid his bicycle down and crept from one tree to another until he was roughly halfway between the sidewalk and the house. The cops had the windows in their cruiser rolled down, and the curious lad was able to overhear their conversation while he watched the house at the same time.

Seconds later, whether it was from the surprise of seeing a light come on in the deserted-looking house or the surprise of hearing the policemen loudly exclaim about that occurrence, an involuntary noise came from some-where deep in Jimmy's throat. When, immediately thereafter, the sound of three gunshots pierced the air, the boy very much wished that he'd just stayed home that evening.

Jimmy watched in fascinated terror as the police officers approached the house. He then crept in, undetected, virtually on the men's heels. The house creaked and moaned as though it were in terrible distress. Jimmy, paralyzed with fear by this point, was still standing frozen in place in the living room when the officers had finished checking the house and were approaching the door to leave.

"What do you think you're doing here?" they asked Jimmy. "Don't you know that you're trespassing?"

But Jimmy was physically incapable of speaking—he was staring, with eyes as wide as saucers, at Superman. The TV hero was standing in the living room, in full Superman dress, smiling down at the excited little boy. The policemen didn't seem aware of the image that had captured Jimmy's full attention, but then, in retrospect, that isn't really surprising. It has long been acknowledged that children can quite often see ghosts even when adults cannot.

Yes, by then TV Superman George Reeves was a ghost. He had died from gunshot wounds at the age of 45 on Tuesday, June 16, 1959, roughly one year before little Jimmy Stein made his second pilgrimage to the house. Officially, the death was deemed to be suicide, but there was strong evidence, even then, that the actor had not taken his own life but had been murdered. Those who tried to prove that serious charge were permanently frustrated in their appeal when the actor's body was destroyed by cremation.

The fact that the actor's spirit has shown itself to Jimmy Stein and others may lend credence to the murder theory. Reeves died during a party at his house. Guests reported that the actor had gone upstairs to go to bed, having apparently instructed his guests to continue the party without him. Moments later, those same guests heard three gunshots ring out from the story above them. They ran to the actor's bedroom but were too late. They found Reeves dead, a smoking gun at his side.

It was the ghostly echo of those fatal shots that Jimmy and the two police officers heard on that summer evening of the next year.

A few months later, the vacant house was sold to settle the deceased actor's estate. Not long after, new occupants moved in. Unfortunately, they didn't stay long. Fear of the ghost they saw—George Reeves, decked out in full Superman regalia, appearing briefly in the bedroom where he died—drove them out.

Even residents of neighboring houses began to see the dead man's image both inside and outside his former home. In the 1980s, while the haunted house on Benedict Canyon Drive was being used as a set for a television show, the ghost made another surprise appearance. Unfortunately, the camera crew was not ready for such an event and the image vanished before they could capture it on film.

In a final ghostly coincidence, *Shoeless Joe*, W.P. Kinsella's novel about a ghostly baseball team, was adapted to a screenplay (it was filmed under the title *Field of Dreams*) in this very house.

Hart and Soul

During initial research for this book, I discovered a couple of enticing leads about ghosts in the former home of silent cowboy film star William S. Hart. The mansion, located northwest of Los Angeles in Santa Clarita, now serves as a museum, which made the possibility of a really good ghost story even stronger, because I have found that museums are frequently haunted. As a result I was very much looking forward to hearing an interesting tale when I made a phone call to the William S. Hart Park and Museum.

My hopes were dashed by the museum staff member who answered the phone. Her monosyllabic reply to my introduction, explanation and inquiry was a most emphatic, "No." This left no room for discussion, but it does leave ghost hunters to wonder about the reported sightings of Hart's image. It is said his ghost was seen on several occasions reading a newspaper in the living room of his former house. In addition, his apparition was reportedly seen in his bedroom, where a witness also noted a shimmering female illusion.

Aside from the vehement denial of the legend, perhaps the most interesting aspect of this haunting is the anecdote about the phantom aroma of freshly brewed coffee wafting through the huge home.

If Hart's museum really isn't home to his spirit, then perhaps the old cowboy star is now enjoying his eternal peace. After all, he certainly worked hard enough during his career in the earthly (and earthy) community of Hollywood to virtually create the genre of the Western movie single-handedly.

Lucy Loves Her Home

For a decade, married entertainers Lucille Ball and Desi Arnaz were television's first couple of comedy. Their shows, *I Love Lucy* and *The Lucy-Desi Comedy Hour*, ruled the airwaves in the 1950s and defined the "situation comedy" long before it was recognized as a distinct art form.

Ball's career had begun as a Ziegfeld Girl in vaudeville, and she launched her movie career as one of the singing, dancing Goldwyn Girls. She was a talented musical performer, but it was her natural ability as a comic that people soon recognized as her most endearing talent. Although never a huge star on the silver screen, Lucy appeared in films with such top comics as Bob Hope and the Marx Brothers. Once she hit TV with her screwball antics, her place in the firmament of legendary comedy stars was assured. Few men or women in the history of show business could do physical comedy as well as Lucille Ball.

Desi Arnaz was a musician but, like his on- and off-screen wife, he had a head for business. As Lucy and Ricky Ricardo, the couple made the *I Love Lucy* show an enormous hit; as Lucille Ball and Desi Arnaz, they formed Desilu Studios to capitalize on the growing television industry and more or less created the lucrative concept of syndicated reruns.

To some degree, the couple's on-screen image paralleled their personal lives. For example, when Lucille Ball became

Lucille Ball

pregnant, so did Lucy Ricardo. However, in the original incarnation of the television show the Ricardo family lived in an apartment. From 1954 on, the real-life Arnaz family home was an impressive house on Roxbury Street in Beverly Hills—a house that Lucy loved. Her neighbors were fellow show business stars, and, more importantly, they were her friends. Both her son and her daughter grew from infancy to adulthood in that home. The house was even used as a backdrop for the occasional *I Love Lucy* episode.

Despite television appearances to the contrary, all was not love and laughter between the real-life couple. Lucille Ball and Desi Arnaz divorced in 1960. She remarried the next year but never left the house she and Desi had moved into so many years before. That house became part of her estate when she died in 1989.

Shortly thereafter, the property that had meant so much to the popular comedian was put up for sale. To the shock of Lucy's neighbors and fans alike, the people who bought the house had no intention of living in it as it was—they had in mind a renovation so massive that it was just short of a complete demolition.

Lucille Ball had been so popular with her peers, her neighbors and her audiences—*and* she had been so closely associated with the house on Roxbury—that this destruction became something of a macabre attraction. As a result, the work crews occasionally toiled away in front of an audience. The only time that the famous redhead's ghost appeared, though, all was quiet on the destruction site.

The sole witness to the ghostly manifestation that day had enjoyed a close friendship with Lucille Ball. He'd been out attending to other matters when it occurred to him to drive past the place where he'd often been entertained. The renovations were well underway and overy few parts of the old place remained intact. As the man stood under clear California skies, possibly saying his last goodbyes to both the house and the woman who had loved it, a movement in the periphery of his vision made him turn his head. There, slowly circling the ruins, was the slightly see-through image of Lucille Ball. She stared at what was left of the house as she walked around it. Then, for just an instant, she turned and looked at her friend.

Despite the fact that the man will not reveal his name for fear of ridicule, he swears to what he saw that day. He'd known the woman well enough in life to be certain not only that he'd seen Lucille Ball's ghostly presence but also that her spirit was badly upset and confused by what lay before her. After briefly maintaining eye contact with her friend, Lucy continued her ghostly patrol around to the other side of the house. At that point, the man lost sight of her and, as far as anyone knows, that poignant moment was the first and last recorded appearance of Lucille Ball in the role of a ghost.

The *Adventures* Continue

From 1952 to 1966, the Nelsons—Ozzie, Harriet, David and Ricky—were like family to the viewers who made up the loyal audience for *The Adventures of Ozzie and Harriet*. The weekly television show became much more than a happy diversion for its fans; it became a cherished institution, a model to which "ordinary" American families should aspire. Of course, the "adventures" of the young and growing Nelson family were created by scriptwriters. So, unlike any real problems the viewers might ever have encountered, the situations plotted by the show's script writers were never so challenging that they couldn't be solved by Harriet's patience, Ozzie's wisdom and the boys' innate goodness. Most importantly, all of this had to be accomplished within the time constraints allowed by the television network. As a result, the world presented on the popular television show was nothing short of idyllic.

Of course, even the Nelsons had a "real life," and, for 25 years much of that life was lived out in a pretty two-story home on Camino Palmero Road in Hollywood. By the time Ozzie Nelson died in 1975, both Ricky and David were adults with their own lives and homes (the story of Ricky's haunted house will follow), but Harriet stayed on in the big house until 1980. During that time, the family occasionally saw Ozzie Nelson's image wandering around the house. It wasn't his ghostly presence that bothered them—it was the fact that the comedian seemed decidedly melancholy.

After five years of living alone in the large (and haunted) house, Harriet Nelson listed the valuable property for sale. The new owners had no sooner moved in than they realized that the house came with something of a paranormal value-added package. At night they often heard footfalls along inside corridors when they knew that all the family members were in bed asleep.

When various amenities of the house began to operate as though they were being controlled by an invisible presence, the family started to pay closer attention. They watched in awe as lights turned on and off by themselves— as did faucets, which would pour water and then turn off when no one was near them. Doors would periodically open and then close again as though an unseen person had walked from one room to another.

And it wasn't just the family members who sensed the ghostly activity. In the summer of 1994, while the house was vacant, a painter was hired to redecorate the place. He had just become used to hearing phantom footsteps walking all around him when he got the distinct impression that he was not alone. Someone, he was quite certain, was in the same room as he. Seconds later the tradesman came face to face with an indistinct, milky white form. The apparition wasn't recognizable as Ozzie Nelson (or anyone else specifically) but the witness came away from the experience positive that he had seen a supernatural being.

At last report, the house that the Nelson family once lived in is still standing. For everyone's sake, both previous and current residents, let's hope that there is an atmosphere of happiness throughout the place once again.

* * *

As mentioned earlier, both David and Rick Nelson grew up, moved away from home and started their own families. The house that Rick and his wife Chris bought was located on Mulholland Drive in the Hollywood Hills. At the time of purchase, they were well aware that Errol Flynn, truly one of Hollywood's "bad boys," had designed and built the home as his "playhouse." Not only was the place enormous but its elaborate floor plan also included a labyrinth of secret passageways lined with peepholes for discreetly viewing areas of the house where guests would have had every right to presume they were in private!

All in all, it was a very strange house. Tracy Nelson, Rick and Chris's daughter, recalled that because the front door was oddly located, the family never used it. "Because of that," she said, "I never really felt that house had a heart. It had no center."

This lack of warmth led to Tracy's habit of going directly to her own bedroom as soon as she came home. Not that there was much respite from uncomfortable feelings in that room; it was known to have been the room assigned to Errol Flynn's teenage lover. Tracy Nelson was convinced that room was haunted, but she knew that the girl who had been involved with Flynn at the time of his death was still alive, so she wondered whose presence it was that she was sensing. Her only clue was that the entity seemed to be a female with rather bad taste in fragrances.

The ghost was quite active. While Tracy watched and listened, the spirit would treat the room as though it was hers, not Tracy's. Nothing terribly troublesome ever occurred, just frequent examples of mundane, daily activities being carried out by someone or something that no one could see. For example, the shower door would open and close, the toilet would flush, window blinds would roll up—all unaided by any force that anyone could see.

Tracy Nelson's attitude to her invisible roommate showed an admirable level of maturity. She regarded the ghost as something of an unusual pet. Her only real disappointment was that when she tried to reciprocate invitations she'd received from friends for sleep-over pajama parties, the other girls always declined. They were not, apparently, as accepting of the Nelson's house haunter as Tracy.

When Chris and Rick Nelson's marriage broke up, Tracy stayed on living in the house with her father. As two people who are fond of one another and are sharing a house will do, Tracy and Rick became quite aware of one another's routines. One night, when Tracy was arriving home from work, she was pleased to notice that the dining room light was on. Better still, she could see the silhouette of a man standing in that room. Naturally, she took this to mean that her father was home. Looking forward to visiting with him, Tracy went into the house and called out to the man. There was no answer. Just seconds later, however, the phone rang. It was Rick Nelson calling home to advise his daughter that he'd been delayed and would not be home until late. When she explained that the dining room light had been on and that she'd seen a man in there, Rick Nelson simply said, "Oh, that's just Errol."

It would seem that "just Errol" still felt territorial about a house that had not been his for some 30 years. As Tracy lay on her bed reading, she listened in horror to what she thought was a rather noisy burglar. Knowing the house as well as she did, the young woman could tell when the intruder had reached the room where Rick Nelson displayed all of his gold records and other awards. She was terrified when she began hearing the sounds of serious destruction in that room. Several hours later, after all the noise had stopped, Tracy felt safe enough to make her way downstairs. She expected to find the first floor, especially her father's study, in ruins. Despite the sounds of destruction that she'd heard over the last hours, there seemed to be nothing out of the ordinary in the house. Well, almost nothing. She found their pet cats in a room that was locked from the inside.

Although relieved that nothing, including her father's cherished awards, had been damaged or stolen, Tracy decided she'd had enough of living in a haunted house. She found herself an apartment and moved out on her own.

No doubt Rick missed having his daughter's company. So did the ghost, apparently; shortly after Tracy left the house on Mulholland Drive, Rick Nelson heard the sounds of destruction that Tracy had described as coming from his first floor study now echoing from what had been Tracy's bedroom. Nelson was so sure that there was an intruder trashing the place that he called the police. They found nothing amiss except that the bedroom door had been locked from the inside and the lights in that room had been turned on. Apart from that, every piece of furniture, every decoration, every trinket was exactly where it had been before the sonic disruption.

In 1985, Rick Nelson died in a plane crash. His violent and premature passing to the other side seemed to have a dramatically negative effect on the quality of the haunting at his home. The spirit, or spirits in that strange home—for Ricky Nelson could by then certainly have joined Errol Flynn in haunting the place—became, according to Tracy, "malevolent." Because Tracy was married and settled in her new life by then, there was little she needed to do at the old family home except clear out some special items. This she did, much to the discomfort of her husband, who was convinced that something evil was present even though he was normally extremely skeptical about the supernatural.

The home stood empty for a while. Unfortunately, youngsters found the large abandoned house to be an excellent party spot. Legend has it that once, when that partying got out of hand, a girl was murdered on the property. Shortly thereafter, a fire tore through the place. Eventually, the charred remains of the house were hauled away and the large property was subdivided. So far, there have been no strange reports from any of the people living in the newer houses on the lots carved out of Errol Flynn's original estate.

Not surprisingly, Tracy Nelson has given some thought to the meaning of all the paranormal events in the house she shared with her father. She's come away convinced beyond any doubt that the place was haunted, but she also wonders if the loud, frightening crashes and bangs were, in some way, forerunners—precognitive warnings that Rick Nelson would die violently. If that thought was correct, the message from beyond was unfortunately too obscure to be of any help as a signal to the living.

Today, we can only hope that the Nelsons, whose television personas meant so much to the audiences of the '50s and '60s, are forever playing desirable roles in their happily ever after.

Pickfair Presences

Destined to become one of the cinema's first superstars, universally known as "America's Sweetheart," Mary Pickford was actually born Gladys Marie Smith in Toronto, Ontario, Canada. She certainly worked hard for her popularity; she made 236 films between 1908 and 1935, and appeared in 51 films in 1909 alone! She was the preferred leading lady of Carl Laemmle and D.W. Griffith, the greatest directors of the silent film era, and she was a shrewd businesswoman to boot, earning top-dollar salaries and producing many of her own films with a degree of control that was simply unattainable for most other stars of the time.

Douglas Fairbanks was one of the first great screen swashbucklers, renowned for performing his own dangerous stunts (years before Jackie Chan!) in his signature roles as pirates and dashing rogues. During a Liberty Bond tour with his friend Charlie Chaplin, he met Mary Pickford at a party and immediately fell in love with her. The two stars were married in 1920; that same year, Pickford, Fairbanks and Chaplin formed United Artist Studios. Douglas and Mary were among the 36 founding members of the Academy of Motion Picture Arts and Sciences, the organization behind the Oscars. Fairbanks served as its first

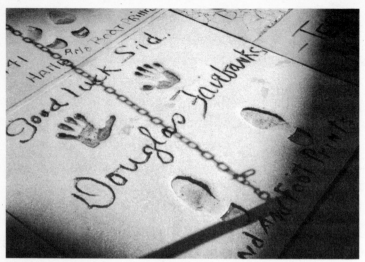

Douglas Fairbanks may have left his hand- and footprints in the cement outside Sid Grauman's Chinese Theatre (now Mann's Chinese Theatre), but his phantom preferred to reside at Pickfair, the mansion he once shared with Mary Pickford.

president, and Mary went on to win a special Lifetime Achievement Oscar of her own in 1976.

If Douglas Fairbanks and Mary Pickford were America's royal couple, then Pickfair, their palatial 42-room mansion, was definitely a castle. Today, only stories remain of the silver screen's fairy tale couple and their haunted home.

When Doug and Mary met in 1915, both of them were already established and enormously popular film stars. They were also both married—to other people. Their attraction to one another was not to be denied, however, and, after two expensive divorces that perhaps foreshadowed many Hollywood break-ups to come, the two lovebirds were finally married.

Fairbanks, who had previously purchased a hunting lodge in Beverly Hills, immediately had the building renovated to become suitable as a home. He gave the property to his beloved Mary as a wedding gift. "Pickfair," as the Pickford/Fairbanks mansion came to be called, was by far the most glamorous home in the area at the time.

The couple took full advantage not only of their standing within the film community but also of their palatial home. They entertained often and splendidly. Being invited to Pickfair was considered a coup—even European royalty hankered to attend soirees there. Once accepted onto the elite guest list, however, everyone had to abide by Mr. and Mrs. Fairbanks's house rules. Perhaps forgetting that they had met and begun a relationship while they were both married to others, the couple deemed that guests who stayed overnight in the mansion could only share a bedroom if they were a married couple.

Out of respect for Doug's adherence to a healthy lifestyle, liquor was never served, and because neither Doug nor Mary ever took time off work, the parties broke up extremely early in the evening. The stars needed to be well-rested for the next day's shooting. Guests who spent the night were expected to turn in early as well; those who were not staying over were expected to leave the property.

It's not known whether any of the Fairbanks's illustrious guests ever saw a ghost in Pickfair, but it is recorded that both Doug and Mary stood and stared in rapt amazement as an apparition of a woman carrying sheet music walked up the main staircase. Who that ghost might have been when she was alive is anyone's guess—possibly the hunting lodge hired musicians to entertain their guests in the evening. In addition, two other ghosts were known to occasionally haunt the house. It was presumed that they, too, had somehow been involved with the building when it was a hunting lodge. They never bothered anyone and actually seemed oblivious to the changes in the facility.

Despite their initial passion for one another, Douglas Fairbanks and Mary Pickford divorced in 1936. Because it had been a gift to her, Mary was awarded possession of Pickfair and, by extension, its ghosts.

The following year Mary Pickford married Buddy Rogers, another actor. The two lived together in Pickfair until Mary's death on May 29, 1979, at which point Rogers moved to one of several outbuildings on the property.

During the tenure of Pickfair's next owner, Mary's ghost—easily recognizable in the little girl-style, ruffled dresses that her characters so often wore—was frequently seen in the main floor den. Doug, who died 40 years before Mary, also returned to haunt his former home. Even in death, he was apparently a friendly and outgoing personality; his image was seen at the front foyer, seemingly prepared to greet another round of honored guests.

Well, Well, Well

The mansion at 1005 North Rexford Drive in Beverly Hills was virtually destined to become a haunted house. Less than a year after actor Clifton Webb bought the large white stucco home in 1947, the place had its first ghost. Happily, that ghost was the spirit of Grace Moore, a woman who had been a friend of Webb's.

Although Moore had been a successful opera singer, she moved to California and enjoyed a second career in movies. By strange coincidence, during the years she was working in Hollywood, Moore also lived for a time in the lovely Spanish-style home that Webb later bought. She was known to have very much enjoyed living in the house and that is no doubt why, after her death in a plane crash, she returned to spend her afterlife in the white stucco bungalow.

When Clifton Webb took up residence in the house, he brought his mother, Maybelle, with him. Both mother and son had an acute interest in the supernatural, and the two regularly held séances in which they warmly contacted their resident spirit. Even when not purposefully communicating with her, the Webbs often saw the figure of a woman dancing in various rooms of the house. The pair always assumed this was the spirit of Grace Moore.

Like Moore, some of Clifton Webb's happiest years were spent at that address. But after his mother died in 1959, Webb became something of a hermit. He enshrined the parts of the house that had been his mother's, preserved all her belongings and maintained daily interactions with the deceased woman via supernatural means.

Webb's unhappiness and anti-social lifestyle after his mother's death may have contributed to his own premature demise in 1966. Not long before he died, the actor told a friend that he loved his house so much that he had no intention of allowing death to keep him from enjoying it. A quick review of reports from people who lived in the house after Clifton Webb's fatal heart attack proves that the man kept his word.

Early in 1967, Joyce and Doug, a couple who were both involved in the movie industry, bought the house. Because Webb's decorating styles had been a reflection of his rather eccentric personality, the new owners needed time before moving in so they could make some changes to the place. Evidence that something about the house was very strange began accruing from the start of those renovations. At first, the incidences were trivial, barely worth noting—a toothbrush left on a bathroom counter later turned up jammed into an electrical receptacle; a pair of contact lenses disappeared and were never found; a door that had been unlocked mysteriously became locked and impenetrable; cigarettes left anywhere in the house were destroyed.

It wasn't until after the couple actually moved into the house that they spotted a flowing, human-shaped form in the window of an empty bedroom. That was when Doug and Joyce began to connect the strange events and to admit to one another that they'd purchased a haunted house.

In a way, that realization might have been a relief for them. In addition to the small annoyances they'd been experiencing, the pair had noted that their dog had been acting oddly; he refused to enter the room they had been told was Clifton Webb's absolute favorite. Instead, the mutt would stand at the doorway, his hackles raised, howling in a highly uncharacteristic way.

Despite the somewhat trying circumstances of sharing their home with a ghost, the couple enjoyed living in the house and wanted to stay. Toward that end, they began to host parties and entertain their friends. Their guests were soon reporting that they too sensed something unusual about the house. One man maintained that as he left the home's master bedroom he suddenly felt the heat drain from the air surrounding him. Other people noticed electric lights going on and off when no one was near the fixture or its switch.

As the months wore on, the couple saw unexplainable shadowy figures in the house and out in the yard, even when there were no guests anywhere on the property. Despite all of this, their determination to keep living at 1005 North Rexford Drive was not shaken until January, 1968, when a real estate agent paid them a surprise visit. It seemed that he had a wealthy client whom he was sure would want to buy the house. More for a lark than in earnest, Joyce and Doug told the agent that they would only be interested in selling at an extremely inflated price. The salesman was soon back to inform them that his customer was willing to meet the couple's price demands.

Although the impromptu real estate transaction had the potential to be extremely lucrative, the owners were unsettled by it. So, apparently, was the previous owner and current ghost of the house. That night, as the woman lay in bed unable to sleep, she watched in rapt fascination as a darkened form moved around her bedroom and a male voice was heard to say, "Well, well, well." The phantom sights and sounds were repeated over the next few days. These experiences left Joyce oddly comforted and gave her a renewed interest in keeping the home.

After some research, she found out that Clifton Webb had a lifelong habit of uttering the phrase, "Well, well, well." Even though the shadowy form they were seeing might have been Grace Moore's ghost, this auditory anomaly seemed to erase all doubt as to the identity of the phantom. Joyce also felt that this was the deceased actor's way of telling her to stay with him in his former home. The next day, apologizing for their apparent indecisiveness, the couple canceled their agreement to sell the haunted house.

After that incident, Clifton Webb's ghost routinely let itself be seen throughout the house and around the yard for varying lengths of time. In the fall of 1968, out of concern for the ghost's happiness, the couple invited a group of psychics to their home to conduct a séance. An entity identifying itself as Clifton Webb quickly began to communicate. He indicated that, in fact, the current owners' impressions were correct: He was a somewhat unsettled spirit. Unfortunately, there didn't seem to be anything that anyone among the living could do to soothe his vexations.

Sadly, Clifton's troubled soul may now be even more upset. The home he could not bear to leave has left him. After Joyce and Doug gave up residency in the house, it was torn down to make room for a more modern home. If the new property owners have ever had any unexpected, unexplainable company, their stories have not yet been made public. Perhaps the phantom has moved on and their new home is a ghost-free zone; since the house was built, there have been reports of Clifton Webb's ghost haunting the area near his grave.

The Barrymore Legacy Endures

The Barrymore acting legacy—which began with Maurice Barrymore's debut on the London stage in 1872, continued with his three children Lionel, Ethel and John Barrymore, trickled down to John's son, John Blyth Barrymore, on to *his* son, John Drew Barrymore, culminating with today's star Drew Barrymore—arguably earns the clan the right to be called America's First Family of Acting. Their family history on the stage and screen goes back an unparalleled four generations. Perhaps it shouldn't be too surprising to learn that stories have emerged surrounding the lives—and the afterlives—of these legendary figures. And one of the best stories about the Barrymores is a classic example of ghostlore.

Despite the fact that it hadn't worked for many years, John Barrymore was extremely fond of a particular cuckoo clock he owned. A short time after Barrymore's death on May 29, 1942, his friend, Gene Fowler, decided to acknowledge the actor's death by setting the hands of this clock to the exact time Barrymore had died. Oddly, he didn't have to make any changes—the clock *already* read 10:20.

The enormous Barrymore estate on Summit Ridge in Beverly Hills was home to considerable spectral activity in the 1970s. Some time after the Barrymores had departed physically, the house was divided into small suites and was almost entirely rented out to various people seeking afford-able accommodation close to the Hollywood careers they hoped to launch. The original owners must not have been pleased with these changes to their home because tenants frequently reported hearing phantom noises from vacant areas of the house. One woman heard a baby crying but was never able to track down the source of the distressing sounds. Although understandably shaken by the experi-ence, she wasn't altogether surprised; she'd also listened to footfalls along apparently empty corridors and within seemingly empty rooms.

Psychics touring the house have sensed that there are at least two ghosts in the house. The male is considerably older than the female. One sensitive felt that there had been a strong emotional connection between the two spirits in life and that, because he had died first, the man had returned to wait for the woman to join him. Many believe that these are the revenants of brother and sister Lionel and Ethel Barrymore.

Rumor also has it that the mansion was used as an ille-gal gambling den at some point after it was sold by the original owners' heirs. In order to conduct their business, these new occupants had telephones installed in most rooms of the house. Those phones are now long gone, but for years afterward the sound of their ringing had tenants jumping up to answer phantom phone calls that had been placed years before.

Not all of the unusual activity was confined to the home itself. A unique feature of the Barrymore estate was a cable car that ran down the side of an embankment on the property. It was used to transport residents and guests to and from the family's swimming pool. Time has clouded the details, but apparently a worker was killed while attending to some routine maintenance of the funicular. His spirit continued to linger long after the lift had been abandoned.

And so the Barrymore legacy, which began in the 1870s on the stage in London, England, continues on in many dimensions even today.

Gangster's Ghost

The name Benjamin Siegel probably won't mean much to most readers. If there's an initial impression made by the name alone, it might be thought to resonate respectability. It shouldn't. Benjamin Siegel, born in Brooklyn, New York, on February 28, 1906, became a vicious gangster who remains much better known as "Bugsy" Siegel. He despised the nickname. No one with an ounce of common sense ever called him "Bugsy" to his face because he was as well known for his explosive and vindictive temper as he was for his dashing, matinee idol good looks.

From Siegel's murderous consolidation of the east coast mobs in 1931 until his own gangland execution in 1947, the gangster's violent method of doing business struck terror in the hearts of both his enemies and the public. His infamy was so great that it even warranted a comment in *Time*, where a journalist acknowledged the handsome and successful criminal as "the most famous mobster of his era." J. Edgar Hoover, longtime director of the FBI, called Siegel "America's most dangerous criminal."

To the world of organized crime, Siegel was a valuable, if volatile, human resource. In 1937, Bugsy moved west to find new markets in which to further his underworld career. California was booming economically and therefore becoming too big a market not to exploit fully. The crime syndicate had already developed interests there in illegal gambling, drug running and blackmailing. Profits from these western-based activities had become significant and Siegel's presence as an overseer was

'Bugsy' Siegel

Public Enemy Benjamin "Bugsy" Siegel was brutally gunned down in this Beverly Hills mansion. His spirit, shocked by the gangland execution, remained in the house for many years.

deemed to be warranted. If one were cynical, it would be tempting to include the pleasant climate and the glamour of Hollywood, which Bugsy loved, as also being influences on his decision to move.

While he was living in California, Siegel journeyed to Las Vegas, Nevada, where, in 1946, he began work on a multi-million dollar hotel-casino to be called The Flamingo. Unfortunately, when arranging some additional financing for this ambitious undertaking, Bugsy may have extended his reach too far—fatally so—by investing $5 million of mob money that rightfully belonged to his colleagues Lucky

Luciano and Meyer Lansky. Bugsy's earthly run ended just before midnight on June 20, 1947, in a beautiful Beverly Hills home leased by his mistress, Virginia Hill.

The palatial home had been reinforced with armor-plated doors to protect the high-living criminal from his many enemies, but even those security precautions were insufficient. Bugsy was shot and killed as he walked in front of the plate-glass living room window. The first of five bullets from a high-powered 30-06 rifle entered his head with such force that one of his eyes was found 15 feet across the room on the tiled floor. The four other bullets slammed into his torso, smashing his ribs and perforating his lungs.

Psychics, and others sensitive to the spirit world, consistently reported feeling the presence of the deceased gangster's ghost in the house. They say that Siegel's moment of panic—when he saw his assailants and realized that the game was up and that he was most certainly going to die— left the spot where he expired severely haunted.

Bugsy's ghostly energy may have dissipated by now. The house has, for many years, been home to people with considerably calmer backgrounds. If there's a Mafia in the afterlife, though, it is likely that Benjamin Siegel's spirit has found it.

Eternal Flame

Actors Robert Taylor and Clark Gable (see The Spirit's Inn chapter, p. 86) were peers in many regards. They worked in movies during the same era, each one playing their natural parts as handsome leading men. They were also both very much in love with their wives.

Robert Taylor married beautiful actress Barbara Stanwyck in 1939. Even though the couple divorced in 1952, Stanwyck continued to love Taylor exclusively. It has been written this way: "Nobody could replace the great love of her life."

Robert Taylor died in 1969, but Barbara Stanwyck lived on until January 20, 1990, when she died at the age of 82. During those 21 years of mourning, she coped by psychically keeping in touch with her beloved Robert on a regular basis. Once she died, rumor had it that the ghosts of both Barbara Stanwyck and Robert Taylor haunted a house off Sunset Boulevard in Beverly Hills where they had held passionate clandestine meetings before their marriage. Theirs was clearly a love so strong that neither divorce nor death could diminish it.

Haunted By Houdini?

In 1874, Mr. and Mrs. Weisz of Budapest, Hungary, welcomed their seventh son to the family. They named the little bundle of joy Ehrich. The Weisz family moved to the United States when Ehrich was four years old, settling in the town of Appleton, Wisconsin. The boy grew up in perfectly ordinary circumstances. His parents weren't wealthy—his father was a rabbi—but the children certainly never did without.

Ehrich Weisz's birth and upbringing may have been unremarkable, but the child was not. His intelligence and sensitivity were exceeded only by his intensely burning ambition. The combination meant that, by the earliest days of the 20th century, this driven young man had become world famous as Harry Houdini, magician extraordinaire.

Houdini's eventual destiny—performing amazing feats of magic on the stages of the world before hundreds of thousands of people—and his route to that pinnacle have become the fascinating subject of articles, books and movies. While a quick review of some of those facts is definitely called for here, I have found, and hope that you will agree, that the feats the great illusionist has performed *after* his physical death are by far the most interesting.

Houdini's introduction to the stage was not a reputable one, but at least he put the things he learned during those early years to good use. The future magician began his career as one of the hundreds of charlatan psychics touring the United States. He was flamboyant and dramatic enough to do well at the scam, but as he told more and more fortunes, Harry Houdini found a strange thing happening to himself. Rather than making up the "readings" for people as he went along, he found that he was actually picking up information that had not been given to him overtly. Completely unintentionally, and much to his distress, Harry Houdini was actually sharpening his intuitive skills. He was becoming, in a word, psychic. The realization unnerved the man so severely that he quit his act as a phony psychic and began to hone his skills as a magician. In that regard, of course, the rest is history.

As a sideline to his extremely popular magic shows, Houdini devoted a great deal of energy to exposing fake psychics—and he had an enormous number of candidates to choose from. The huge number of deaths occasioned by the First World War and the flu epidemic that swept the world in 1918 meant that a great many people were grieving. Spiritualism, especially as a means of contacting those who had died, became popular all over the world. Unfortunately, it also became a field full of crooks who took whatever money they could pilfer from bereaved families in exchange for a well-orchestrated "visit" with the dearly departed loved ones. Perhaps to ease his conscience over the time he'd spent in this shady field, Harry Houdini issued a challenge to practicing psychics everywhere, announcing that he would replicate, with magic, any of the stunts that they labeled as supernatural.

With that gauntlet dropped, Harry Houdini went on

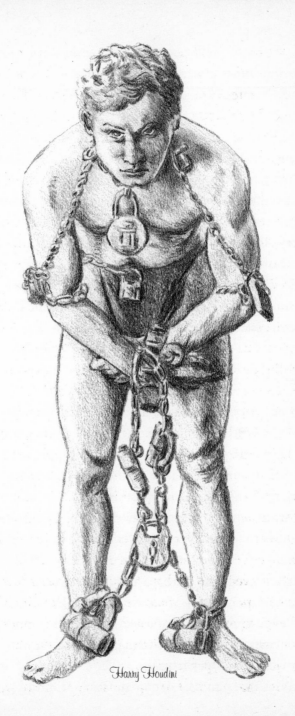

Harry Houdini

sharpening his skills as a magician and escape artist. His accomplishments were nothing short of amazing. By perfecting his timing and mastering breath control, the man entertained audience after audience as he escaped from handcuffs, safes, trunks and coffins. By working constantly and obsessively, Houdini learned how to tap his natural powers to the point that his abilities seemed almost supernatural when compared to those of the average person. And the more capable he became in the world of illusion and escape, the more skeptical he became about the supposed world of spiritualism and the spirits.

Houdini was touring Los Angeles in April of 1923 when a man named Albert H. Hetzel contacted him. The information Hetzel had for Houdini seemed likely to prove, once and for all, whether or not a paranormal world actually existed. The previous July, a woman named Mary Fairfield McVickers celebrated her 73rd birthday. During the celebrations, Mrs. McVickers made an announcement.

"I have had a vision of my approaching death," she informed her guests. "I believe that if a photograph is taken over my body about 5:00 PM on the day of my funeral, I will appear in the picture in spirit form."

At the time, all those gathered assured the woman that she'd live to see many more birthdays, but just nine months later, Mary Fairfield McVickers was dead. After alerting Houdini, Hetzel also gathered together Larry Semon, a movie producer, and Nathan Moss, an expert in photography. The four men, equipped with the latest in that era's camera technology, entered the church where Mrs. McVickers' body lay in a coffin. Beginning precisely at 5:00 PM, they took 10 photographs in approximately three minutes.

All but the second shot revealed nothing more than the scene that lay before the men—the woman's inert body in her coffin. The second exposure, however, showed a strange streak of light just above the corpse. The anomaly stretched nearly to the ceiling, narrowing as it rose until it became a "diffused luminous mass." Neither Houdini nor any of the others could offer any explanation for the oddity. This experience, combined with the personal psychic experiences that had unnerved him so badly as a youth, convinced Houdini that he had proof of a world beyond ours.

On another occasion, Houdini carefully inspected some very strange baby pictures from Blackhawk, Colorado, taken during the late 1800s by a pioneer in the world of photography named Alexander Martin. Upon close examination, the seemingly ordinary photographs taken by Martin showed not only the child who had been photographed but also the less distinct faces of children who had not been present at the sitting—perhaps the ghosts of little ones who had died before their time but had not yet fully left our plane.

Throughout these experiences, Houdini was becoming more and more firm in his beliefs about the supernatural. Thinking that he was in perfect health and would live for many more years, the magician made a pact with his wife. He promised her that when he died, if there was indeed a life after death, he would return to her. At the time, no one had any idea that Houdini's days were numbered.

Because he was the consummate showman, Harry Houdini kept a stock of publicity photographs featuring himself in costume. During his long show business career, he had given away hundreds of these pictures, usually autographed. One of those photos was the proud possession of magician Robert F. Gysel. Gysel wrote an interesting letter to a friend of Houdini's named Fulton Oursler. The letter stated, "Houdini had given me a picture of himself which I had framed and hung on the wall. On October 24th, 1926, at 10:58, the picture fell to the ground, breaking the frame." This, Gysel informed Oursler, was a forerunner—a predictor of Houdini's imminent death.

Because Houdini was performing in Detroit at the time and Gysel was at his home in Toledo, the lesser magician would have had no idea that the world's greatest illusionist was indeed unwell with peritonitis at the time. Exactly one week later, on Halloween 1926, Harry Houdini spoke his last words: "I'm tired of fighting. I guess this thing is going to get me." Then he died. His widow's vigil for contact with Houdini from beyond the grave had begun.

Whether or not Beatrice Houdini ever received that word has been a controversial issue since January 9, 1929, when she signed an affidavit confirming that his spirit had come through to her and communicated in a code that the two had devised. Soon after that, and for the rest of her life, Houdini's widow waffled, not in her conviction that the correct message came through, but that it was her husband who had sent it.

Many believe that Beatrice Houdini's public wavering, even though Harry had kept his part of their pact by following the plan exactly, is the source of the frustration that has kept Houdini's spirit from resting. As a matter of fact, nothing is easy about this ghost story.

An estate at the corner of Laurel Canyon Boulevard and Willow Glen Road was recently listed for sale as "the estate known as Harry Houdini's." Even in Houdini's day, real estate transactions left an easy-to-follow paper trail, so it would seem a simple matter to verify whether or not the magician ever resided at that address. That has not been the case. Neither the name Harry Houdini nor Ehrich Weisz shows up anywhere on the official records for that piece of land. The first house built on the four-acre lot was a veritable mansion built in the early 1920s for a Los Angeles businessman named R.J. Walker. That house and the outbuildings associated with it burned to the ground in the 1950s.

Why then would anyone connect the ruins of that original structure with Houdini? The short answer to the question is that this is the location where Houdini's ghost appears most often. In addition to seeing an apparition, a "dark phantom" believed to be that of the deceased magician's, people have also witnessed ghost lights and phantom sounds around the rubble that was once the staircase as well as mysterious footsteps in a garden grotto on the property.

While cleaning up the landscaping around the property in 1998, the current owner, an antique dealer from Georgia, found the remains of iron gates. The year 1919, as well as two names had been engraved into the metal. "Walker" was one of those names and "Houdini" was the other.

If it *was* the skeptical magician haunting the West Hollywood estate, then he must have had company there, because people have also reported seeing a ghostly woman in green lingerie hovering in approximately the same area. It's nice to think that Houdini's ghost may have had a companion during the years he spent trying to convince his widow of his continuing presence. But somehow it's even more reassuring to hope that Beatrice has experienced the reality of life after death first-hand after her own passing and that she and Harry are happily reunited in spirit.

Valentino— The Sheik of Ghosts

Some movie stars have remained larger than life long after their deaths. Silent film's favorite leading man, Rudolph Valentino, is certainly one of those. Handsome and dashing, Valentino was one of Hollywood's first "heart-throbs." Women all over the world adored him. Just to get a glimpse at the man, they flocked to his movie premieres and even to his home, forcing him to protect his property and himself with surrounding walls, floodlights, security guards and trained dogs. These were lofty heights for an ambitious young man who left his middle-class upbringing in Italy in 1913 to immigrate to New York City, where he began work as a paid dance partner in a cocktail lounge.

By 1917 he had managed to get himself hired as a dancer in the chorus of a play heading from New York to California. Valentino's timing must have been exquisite both on and off the dance floor, because his arrival in Hollywood coincided nearly perfectly with the explosion in the number of movies being filmed there. Valentino's ambitions of a glamorous career were about to be realized. Although only a dance extra, his first screen appearance created tremendous excitement among audiences—especially the women in those audiences. Few had seen the kind of sensuality that this young man flaunted. That first, otherwise unforgettable silent movie meant that

Rudolph Valentino

Rudolph Valentino's tango to fame, fortune and an early death had begun.

Over the next nine years, Valentino made a string of films and developed a loyal following of passionate fans. Some were so enthralled by their idol that the announcement of his death at the age of 31 on August 23, 1926, caused mass hysteria and even suicides. The public grieving had not yet begun to calm down when, only three days later, the first reports of his ghostly presence began to surface. Fan magazines carried transcripts of his ghostly messages in their next editions.

Valentino's widow, Natacha Rambova, lost no time in contacting a trance medium named George B. Wehner. Together they were able to communicate with the deceased, who indicated that he was not at all pleased to have died when he did. He told the pair of his extreme frustration at being cut off in the prime of his life and of his first futile attempts to reconnect and interact with the living. The disembodied spirit spoke of his frustrating efforts to return to places and people he'd known in life, only to realize that the living were completely unaware of his presence. For a man who was once recognized worldwide, this must have been difficult to understand and accept. Perhaps his spirit never learned to overcome that change, because there have been sightings of Rudolph Valentino's ghost in many different places.

Valentino's main residence, Falcon's Lair, took its name from a long-planned movie, to be called *The Hooded Falcon*. Natacha Rambova had written the screenplay and intended for her husband to play the lead character. Sadly, he didn't live long enough to make the film. The pet project's importance to the couple, however, is clearly reflected in the name chosen for their treasured estate.

By current standards, the house would probably be considered garish. But in its day, Falcon's Lair was seen as the height of luxury. "Extravagant" and "palatial" were two words most commonly used to describe the massive Mediterranean mansion situated on a hilltop overlooking Beverly Hills. In addition to the house itself, there were outbuildings: stables, garages and housing for the servants who tended both to the eight acres of land and the owners' prized animals.

Shortly after the star's death, a stable hand fled in terror after walking into the horse barns and seeing the phantom image of Valentino carefully grooming a steed that had been a particular favorite. The worker never returned to his haunted place of employment. People visiting the pet cemetery in Los Angeles that is the final resting place of Kabar, Valentino's beloved Great Dane, have watched in fascination as the ghostly pup's spirit plays among the grave markers.

Harry Carey, Valentino's coyly named friend and fellow actor, attested that he had seen the readily recognizable wraith prowling the halls and rooms of Falcon's Lair. The image had not disturbed Carey in any way, but an actress who tried to spend the night in the home maintained that she was chased out by the ghost. Like the stable hand before her, she ran from the property vowing never to return to the haunted house.

Valentino's attachment to Falcon's Lair was so strong that his image has even manifested to people who were simply walking past the place. Over the years, passersby have been taken aback by the sight of the former owner's ghost staring out from a second floor window.

In order to settle the actor's estate, his beloved home was put up for sale. A haunted mansion, however, can be a difficult piece of property to unload. Legend has it that many prospective buyers expressed interest in the place but, after touring it, never returned. In one instance, a deal was in progress when the potential purchaser quite uncharacteristically backed out. Perhaps he, like others, heard the echoes of phantom footfalls along empty corridors of the huge home.

But Falcon's Lair is not the only place that the matinee idol's ghost has haunted. In 1921, while he was filming *The Sheik*, Rudolph Valentino lived in a beach house at Oxnard, just north of Los Angeles. After his death, the porch area of this house became haunted by a "dark phantom." This ghost, which paces back and forth, seems oblivious to the living and is presumed to be another manifestation of Valentino's leftover energy.

During his career, Valentino never fully adjusted to his enormous popularity. Although he often expressed doubt about the extent of his status as a celebrity, he did recognize the need to seek refuge from his adoring fans. One of his hideaways was a quaint inn at Santa Maria, California. Guests who have since stayed in the room that Valentino always rented suspect that the inexplicable sounds and unnerving feelings of an unseen presence are caused by his ghost. When that presence seems to be on the bed with them, guests are understandably perturbed.

The former lady-killer must not have lost his peacock-like interest in flashy clothes, because he's been seen several times in the wardrobe department of Paramount Studios. Witnesses report that Valentino's image appears as a shimmering form in the area where old garments are stored. He doesn't bother anyone, but just seems content to be in his beloved studio environment.

Rudolph Valentino, the ambitious young immigrant who arrived in Hollywood just in time, seems to have no intention of leaving—even though it has now been more than 70 years since his death!

Act **2**

HOLLYWOOD

The Spirit's Inn

Playbill

Montgomery Clift (1920-1966)

Red River (1948)

A Place in the Sun (1951)

I Confess (1953)

From Here to Eternity (1953)

Raintree Country (1957)

Suddenly, Last Summer (1959)

The Misfits (1961)

Judgment at Nuremberg (1961)

Carmen Miranda (1909-1955)

Down Argentine Way (1940)

That Night in Rio (1941)

Weekend in Havana (1941)

Springtime in the Rockies (1942)

Doll Face (1945)

Copacabana (1947)

Nancy Goes to Rio (1950)

Scared Stiff (1953)

Marilyn Monroe (1926-1962)

Monkey Business (1952)

How to Marry a Millionaire (1953)

Niagara (1953)

Gentlemen Prefer Blondes (1953)

The Seven Year Itch (1955)

Bus Stop (1956)

The Prince and the Showgirl (1957)

The Asphalt Jungle (1957)

Some Like It Hot (1959)

The Misfits (1961)

Humphrey Bogart (1899-1957)	Carole Lombard (1908-1942)
The Petrified Forest (1936)	Big News (1929)
Dead End (1937)	No Man of Her Own (1932)
Angels with Dirty Faces (1938)	Twentieth Century (1934)
The Roaring Twenties (1939)	My Man Godfrey (1936)
The Maltese Falcon (1941)	Swing High, Swing Low (1937)
Casablanca (1942)	Nothing Sacred (1937)
To Have and Have Not (1944)	Made for Each Other (1939)
The Big Sleep (1946)	Mr. and Mrs. Smith (1941)
The Treasure of the Sierra Madre (1948)	To Be or Not to Be (1942)
Key Largo (1948)	
The African Queen (1951)	
Sabrina (1954)	
Beat the Devil (1954)	
The Caine Mutiny (1954)	

Clark Gable (1901-1960)

The Painted Desert (1931)

No Man of Her Own (1932)

Strange Interlude (1932)

It Happened One Night (1934)

Mutiny on the Bounty (1935)

The Call of the Wild (1935)

China Seas (1935)

Cain and Mabel (1936)

San Francisco (1936)

Gone with the Wind (1939)

Across the Wide Missouri (1951)

The King and Four Queens (1956)

The Misfits (1961)

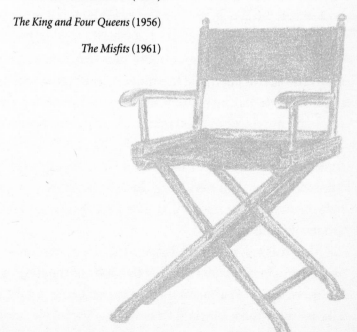

Some Stars Never Checked Out

From its earliest days, the Hollywood Roosevelt Hotel played an important role in the film industry and the lives of movie stars. In 1929, Douglas Fairbanks presided over the first-ever Academy Awards ceremony when hundreds of Hollywood pioneers gathered in the hotel's Blossom Room. Since then, the Roosevelt has hosted glittering, star-studded parties and has often been regarded as *the* place to be seen. Even today, phantom echoes of those events continue to reverberate throughout the palatial inn.

Little is known about the ghosts in the hotel prior to the first recorded encounters in 1985, just before the hotel's grand reopening after a mammoth two-year, $40-million renovation. During mid-December in 1985, everyone at the Roosevelt was busy preparing for the upcoming day when the hotel would once again receive guests. No matter what their usual duties or job titles, all employees were directly involved with the last-minute details—secretaries were sweeping, bellmen were dusting, waitresses were helping make up guest rooms. The place was a veritable model of industry.

Alan Russell, personal assistant to the general manager, was painstakingly sweeping the floor of the Blossom Ballroom in anticipation of the new carpet being installed. Like many of those on staff, Russell was a part-time actor; given the star-studded history of the hotel, the "day job"

The Hollywood Roosevelt Hotel is home to the stars—dead or alive.

was very much a labor of love. Being able to devote some of himself to this gorgeous room that had been so important to the history of movie-making felt more like a privilege than a chore. It was also a perfect time, he thought, "to commune with the spirits of those who received Academy Awards here."

As Alan's experience unfolded, it became a far closer encounter than he had anticipated. The room is large and the job had to be done thoroughly, so Alan was taking his time and making sure he didn't miss any part of the floor. After repeatedly going back over to a certain area in the ballroom, he realized that while the rest of the room was kept at a very comfortable temperature, the air in that particular spot was incredibly chilly.

More puzzled than concerned, Alan called in a fellow employee, Kelly Greene. He hoped that together they could determine what was causing the anomaly. They didn't succeed in finding an explanation, but they did document the strange physical properties of the area. The cool spot is a circle about 30 inches in diameter, in which the temperature is inexplicably 10 degrees cooler than anywhere else in the room. Every logical cause for this oddity was checked, but to no avail. Since then, visiting psychics have explained that the cold spot is caused by the ghost of "a man wearing black." The psychics added that they detected "a lot of anxiety" in that one small area. Perhaps the tension felt by one of the first Oscar nominees has left its mark on the atmosphere.

While Alan Russell was puzzling over the strange situation in the ballroom, another employee, Suzanne Leonard, was dusting in the general manager's office. One of the pieces of furniture there was a tall, dark-framed mirror. As Suzanne wiped her cloth over the reflective glass, she was shocked to see the face of a young blond woman staring back at her. Suzanne had assumed that she was alone in the room, so she swung around to see who had joined her. There was no one else in the office, and therefore no way

A portrait of Marilyn Monroe—who haunts the mirror on the next wall—is between those of Jean Harlow and Vivian Leigh. Of the three stars, only Leigh seems to rest in peace.

that anyone's face could've been reflected in the mirror. She turned back to the mirror. The image was still there.

That was enough for Suzanne! She left her chore and went in search of the man whose office she'd been cleaning. According to information released by the hotel, the general manager "told her that the mirror had belonged to Marilyn Monroe and had been removed from the suite out by the pool that Marilyn had often occupied." While those in authority at the hotel are understandably hesitant to state that the long-dead movie legend haunts the mirror, they do report that "two psychics have 'read' the mirror and told of seeing great sadness [in it]." Management has since moved the mirror to a spot where it is more accessible to visitors. They invite those passing to "take a look—you may see a blond reflection." (When psychic Peter James investigated

This mirror once decorated Marilyn Monroe's favorite suite.
Psychics say they have seen her ghostly image peering out at them from
the reflective glass.

that same mirror, it revealed a "pretty, dark-haired woman" who gave her name as Dee Rio, but the image vanished before he could learn anything about her.) Marilyn Monroe's presence in the hotel is not restricted to sightings in the mirror. The sex symbol's image has also been detected by the pool that is located near the Tropicana Bar. It is also said that Betty Grable, Gypsy Rose Lee and Ethel Merman have left their psychic imprints in that part of the hotel.

Before the Roosevelt's reopening, more than just the Grand Ballroom and the manager's offices had to be cleaned. Guest rooms also had to be readied for occupancy, and that is what a team of workers was busy doing on the ninth floor when a woman who usually worked as a waitress in the hotel's dining room had a paranormal encounter. At first, she didn't recognize it as such—she thought that the rather sudden cool breeze she felt in Room 928 was only a draft. After all, there were others working up on that floor, and it was perfectly reasonable to think that one of them might have left a door or a window open near that room.

The woman put the incident out of her mind until she walked back into the room to stock it with towels. As soon as she stepped inside the room, the door forcefully slammed shut behind her. Not only was this startling, but the implications were also extremely unnerving to the woman—she knew for a fact that the doors to *all* guest rooms in the hotel operated on compression hinges, making it physically impossible for any of them to slam. Even so, she knew what she'd heard.

Understandably anxious to have other people near her, the woman rushed out into the hallway. As she did, she felt

Room 928 in the Hollywood Roosevelt Hotel is thought to be haunted by the ghost of Montgomery Clift.

the cool draft again; then, while making her way down the hall, she felt something ice cold brush past her. This woman was no doubt thankful that her usual waitressing job with the hotel would rarely, if ever, require her to be in Room 928 again!

Two other female employees didn't have that luxury. After explaining to their supervisor that they felt "something strange" in Room 928, the pair absolutely refused to enter the room ever again.

This ninth-floor corridor is where Montgomery Clift paced while memorizing his lines for the movie From Here to Eternity. *It is said that his spirit never left.*

Hotel records show that Montgomery Clift rented Room 928 while he was filming the classic movie *From Here to Eternity*. During those months, he apparently had a habit of pacing up and down the corridor while memorizing his lines. What a shame the hotel workers who were so startled couldn't have known that they were possibly in the presence of one of the most handsome movie stars the world has ever known—they might have felt honored rather than frightened!

Montgomery Clift

Despite these bits of interference from beyond, the Hollywood Roosevelt Hotel reopened for business in a limited capacity just before New Years Eve in 1985—only rooms on the third, fourth and fifth floors were ready for occupancy. For this reason, the hotel's switchboard operator was surprised to receive a phone call, at exactly midnight, from a room on the tenth floor. The operator answered the call, but found no one on the line. As the hotel later explained, that lack of response was "for good reason"—the room from which the call originated had not been refurbished or rented out, so there was no phone in the room!

A telephone in at least one room on the twelfth floor of the Roosevelt has also given the switchboard operators trouble. The particular room is one that famed astrologer and author Linda Goodman rented in 1959 while writing one of her books. During her stay, Goodman indicated that there was "a presence, a special quality" about that room.

According to records at the Roosevelt, "In October of 1989, that presence made itself known again by telephone." Late one night, Room 1221 lit up on the switchboard. The operator responded, but there was no one on the line. When the light lit up again, the operator double-checked the guest register and found that the room was not occupied. She called Security, explained the situation, and asked that someone check the room and put the phone back on the hook. Security responded, and that was that—until three nights later, when it happened again. This time, the phone got off the hook "by itself" three times in one hour. Each time, Security went up to the room and returned the handset to its cradle; the next time they went up, the phone would again be off the hook.

All of this in an unoccupied, locked room.

As the months went by, more and more floors of the hotel opened up to guests. One day in spring of 1986, Daniel Cichon, Assistant Director of Housekeeping, was giving some of the rooms a final inspection. As he left a suite he'd been inspecting on the eleventh floor, Cichon turned off the lights and locked the door. Moments later, he came back to the rooms, unlocked the door, and was quite startled to find all the lights on.

At about the same time Cichon had his strange experience, Rachel, a lobby maid at the hotel, was restocking her cart with supplies from a storage cupboard. As she reached in to pick out the items she needed, something unseen gave her a firm push into the closet. Assuming that it was just a fellow employee teasing her, Rachel yelled for him to "cut it out." Seconds later, Rachel whirled around to face the prankster—and was horrified to realize that there was no one anywhere near her.

Phantom sounds are also heard in that area of the hotel. The administration reports receiving "calls from guests, late at night, complaining about loud conversations in the next room—but when Security investigates, they find the next room unoccupied." The hotel has also received "calls about people talking loudly in the halls late at night, but Security has never found anyone out there."

More than willing to accept practical explanations for such noises, the management of the hotel acknowledges that "all old buildings creak and moan now and then." However, they also acknowledge that the number of calls they receive about the phantom noises is probably too high for them all to be chalked up to a settling structure—they have received four or five of these calls each month since the hotel reopened.

In November of 1989, a guest called the switchboard to complain about "kids being loud in the room next door." The employee who answered the call assured the guest that there was no one in the next room. "A little later, the same lady called again, this time very insistent that 'those kids are still loud and they *are* next door.'" The switchboard operator dispatched a member of the hotel's security force to investigate. The room was found to be unoccupied.

These sorts of complaints continued for a few years. Some people even mentioned "strange shadows." Neither the noises nor the shadows were ever explained to the satisfaction of ghost enthusiasts.

Two and a half years after the hotel's reopening, an employee named Steve Fava, who was responsible for filling the pop machines in the halls, went about his task. Steve carried a clipboard which held the paperwork for the job. As he moved from floor to floor, stocking the machines, he would put the clipboard on top of the pop dispenser, well within easy reach.

Just as he had the last can of soda loaded into one machine and was ready to head off to fill the next, Steve discovered that his clipboard was no longer where he'd left it. After a thorough search, the puzzled man found his clipboard inside the ice machine, "an arm's length away from the soda machine."

Being a practical sort, Steve "decided he must have put it on the ice machine and [that] it had just slipped off and into the ice." His resolve was somewhat shaken, however, when "on the next floor, it happened again"—and then "on each floor it happened." By the time he reached the 10th floor, Steve was badly shaken and took extra care to be sure to put the clipboard on the soda machine. Once again, he finished stocking the sodas and reached for the clipboard; once again, it was gone. After a great deal of hunting, Steve finally found the clipboard—it was inside the ice machine that time, too.

The rest of the report on that incident indicates that Steve, "his face white with fright, raced to the general manager's office and said, 'Don't ever make me do that again! I swear those machines are haunted.'"

Hotels employ security guards to keep watch over the property. Normally, where surveillance is concerned, the "buck stops" with those employees. At the Hollywood Roosevelt, however, the ghosts keep a watchful eye out for the guards.

In the fall of 1989, several new security guards were hired. One guard, perhaps an especially sensitive person, reported feeling that he was being watched. Upon careful inspection, he determined that no one else was in the area. Even so, he would suddenly feel uncomfortable and would hurry down the hall, hoping to see another person. He never did. Oftentimes it would feel like someone had been standing in the next doorway but had suddenly stepped back inside the room just as he approached. The guard didn't see or hear anything—it was just something that he sensed.

The hotel even has its own "ghost writer." As a release issued by the hotel indicates, "Late one night in September of 1989, the Night Supervisor of Housekeeping was passing the Personnel Office and heard the electric typewriter being used. Knowing that the staff leaves at 5:00 PM, she knocked on the door to see who was in the office. There was no response. Several times she knocked and called out, but there was still no response—only the steady tap-tap-tapping of the typewriter. Next morning, when the personnel staff arrived, the typewriter was still turned on, a chair that had been left at a desk was now arranged in front of the typewriter, and the papers on all of the desks had been neatly arranged."

More recently, Sales Coordinator Karen Bookholt got a real surprise when she entered her own office early one July morning. Her keyboard was, as she put it, "typing all by itself." When Karen expressed her alarm, the typing stopped. After taking a deep breath, the woman informed whatever force was at work, "That's okay, you can keep typing." The activity resumed. What a shame that there wasn't any paper in the typewriter either time. A legible message from beyond would certainly have been intriguing!

Ghosts and electrical equipment have often proved to be a volatile combination, and this was certainly the case when a film crew came into the Roosevelt to shoot a documentary about the resident spirits just before Halloween of 1989. Each time the camera operators moved to the corridor outside Room 928, where Montgomery Clift's spirit is thought to be present, lights would inexplicably go out. (Another time, when a crew from the television show *Entertainment Tonight* tried to film a segment in that same room, a camera operator's light actually exploded.) Sound recording equipment broke down while the operators were trying to work on another floor, and when the team moved to the ballroom, the audio equipment was also affected—but only within the cold spot.

At another point in the shoot—and for no reason that anyone could discern—film jammed in the cameras. Perhaps the most interesting moment in the filming ordeal came when the crew set up to capture some footage of a particular mirror—the mirror that had once belonged to Marilyn Monroe. Seconds into shooting the scene, something triggered the alarm in a nearby smoke detector. The crew never did get that shot recorded.

A psychic entering the Roosevelt's Cinegrill room had news for the staff. She announced that she sensed "a very strong presence" in the room. "There's a ghost here," she maintained. "It's a man, a black man—a musician. He plays a clarinet." Prior to the psychic's visit, no one had known of the existence of that particular entity.

The following two incidents, both actual sightings of an apparition, occurred within 48 hours of each other. During the evening of Saturday, December 15, 1990, the Los Angeles County District Attorney's office held their annual holiday dinner and dance in the haunted hotel. As the successful night of celebrating wore down, one of the guests and his wife were enjoying a look at the photographs that adorn the walls of the mezzanine level.

The couple made their way along the display until they came to the area where the mezzanine overlooks the Blossom Room. At that point, they were surprised to hear piano music. Intrigued, the pair followed the sound of the music until they found a piano. Although there was no one playing the instrument, there was a man dressed in a white suit standing beside it. According to hotel records, "the couple spoke to him, but he didn't answer." Then, to add to the couple's confusion, "as they got closer,

Marilyn Monroe's ghost has been seen at the Hollywood Roosevelt's pool, located near the Tropicana Bar. Other spirits seen in this area include those of Betty Grable, Gypsy Rose Lee and Ethel Merman.

the man disappeared. He didn't walk away, he vanished!"

When psychic Peter James investigated in March of 1992, he felt the Blossom Room was "clear of ghosts," but "he felt the impressions of people who had been there often in the hotel's early days." Errol Flynn, Betty Grable and Edward Arnold were three of those whose physical presence had left a mark on the psychic atmosphere of the room many years before.

The next sighting was made by an employee the following Monday. Information released by the hotel indicates that the employee involved in this encounter, a man named Billy, is "from the Philippines—a culture that firmly believes in spirits."

Humphrey Bogart

Billy was walking along a third-floor hallway when he came to a corner. As he looked to his left, he saw a man standing about halfway down the hall. Thinking the man was lost or in need of some kind of assistance, Billy called out to him. The man didn't answer, but because he kept looking from side to side as if he wasn't sure which way to go, the concerned employee approached him. "Billy came closer, within three feet of the man, and again asked if he could be of help. The man still did not reply but turned and walked toward the fire exit at the east end of the hall. Then he walked through the door! He didn't open it and walk out—he went through the door! Billy tried to follow, but his feet were rooted to the spot."

Billy later acknowledged that, while it felt as though he was paralyzed with fear by the experience for five minutes, in reality "it was probably only a few seconds." It would be interesting to arrange a meeting between Billy and the couple who'd seen the manifestation of a man in white standing by the piano. Billy also described the ghost that he saw as wearing a white suit, but that does not necessarily mean it was the same manifestation.

That man in white was probably not the same ghost that a desk clerk saw. According to hotel reports, clerk Troy Robertson was counting receipts one spring night when "he was startled to see a man walk past him and into the next room. Actually, he was mostly shocked because the man had no face! After a moment of near-panic, Troy cautiously stepped into the doorway to see if there really was a man in the room. There was absolutely no one there—and there is no other way in or out of that room." The incident unnerved the employee so badly that he no longer wishes to discuss the experience.

When psychic researcher Peter James investigated the haunted hotel, he had complete cooperation—from both the management of the inn and its ghosts. "At the end of a hallway on the third floor, he received the impression of Carmen Miranda, and near the elevator he felt the presence of Humphrey Bogart. In the Academy Room (originally the hotel's library and a meeting place for civic groups and social clubs), Peter encountered the spirit of a little girl— Carol or Caroline—who was looking for her mother. Others had reported seeing a similar ghost, such as the hotel employee who described a "child about five years old, with light brown hair pulled back in a ponytail, wearing a light pink jacket and little blue jeans. She was so cute, skipping around the fountain and singing." The image may have been appealing, but it certainly wasn't permanent. Seconds later, it vanished.

There was an extremely cold spot in the Academy Room which Peter described as a tubular shaft where the spirits enter. This, he felt, was "their gathering place."

The report continued, "In the dark recesses of the old Arthur Murray Dance Studio that adjoins the hotel, Peter felt many spirits, especially on the stairway." More intriguing still is the fact that the stairway in question backs onto an outside wall of the Academy Room—a spot that James had identified as "hiding something valuable of historic significance."

On April 26, 1992, Peter James's camera operator, a man identified only as "Dimtri," filmed the psychic in an amazing battle against an aggressive entity. The entourage was up in the penthouse when Peter "was suddenly grabbed about the legs" by an invisible force. As Peter struggled to free himself and to communicate with the entity, Dimtri continued to let his camera run. The result was a riveting and dramatic clip of film that clearly showed the psychic struggling against an unseen attacker. Through it all, Peter talked to the manifestation and eventually calmed it. The presence, he informed Dimtri, was a former bodyguard named Frank. It would seem that the spirit's desire to protect the area did not die with his physical body.

The last place in the hotel that Peter James and his entourage explored was the basement, which he initially declared to be "clean" of ghosts. Seconds later, however, the psychic sensed the spirit of a woman who had once been employed by the hotel. As the entity communicated with Peter, sheets that were hung over a "high rod … began to undulate." The movement stopped and Peter realized that the spectral presence was no longer in the room. He stepped toward the area where he'd sensed her just a moment before—and found that it was icy cold.

For the most part, the management and staff at the Hollywood Roosevelt Hotel take the extra "guests" at the establishment in stride. This is probably just as well, because it would seem that the hotel continues to be important to movie stars—even those who are long gone.

Gable & Lombard Forever

Throughout the history of the film industry, movie stars have loved Hollywood. They've loved the community, the camaraderie, the work and, of course, the wealth and recognition they've gained from their association with film production. This intensity, however, sets up an occasional but understandable need for those same actors to escape from the town and all it represents—in other words, the necessity to take holidays. Today, Hollywood's biggest stars own recreation homes in many of the most desirable areas of the world and take a break from their grueling work schedule and the pressures of their careers by visiting those "homes-away-from-home."

Back in the 1930s, the hideaways were neither so exotic nor so far-flung. For example, when the beautiful Carole Lombard and the handsome Clark Gable decided to "tie the knot" on March 29, 1939, they did so in the quiet hamlet of Kingman, Arizona, not far from the California border. In order to continue maintaining their privacy, Lombard and Gable decided to stay in the area for a few days. Mr. and Mrs. Gable rented a room in a nondescript two-story hotel in nearby Oatman, Arizona where they apparently thoroughly enjoyed consummating their marital union.

For years afterward, both Carole and Clark spoke of that honeymoon as "the time of their lives." What dignity and decorum prevented them from speaking of directly was the physical delight they enjoyed during their stay. While in Oatman, their "superstar" status did not interfere in any way. It was, refreshingly, a non-issue in these backwoods towns. Clark Gable and Carole Lombard, desperately in love with one another, had freedom in Oatman that they never would have had in Hollywood. And they took full advantage of the opportunities this anonymity provided.

Just three years later, in a tragedy so devastating that it could have been ripped from the pages of a melodramatic movie script, a plane carrying Lombard crashed just outside Las Vegas, killing the actress, her mother and 20 other passengers. Carole had been on her way back to California after appearing at a bond rally in her home state of Indiana in support of America's war effort. Gable, who was normally a patriotic man, had argued with his wife before she left. He begged her to make an exception this time and stay home. Their last words to one another were angry ones. As the couple parted, Lombard took off a gold and topaz earring that she'd been wearing to complement her light-colored suit. She threw the trinket, which had been a gift from Gable, at her husband.

Optimistically chalking this up as a quarrel, one they would patch up when Carole returned home, Clark Gable put the single earring in his pocket and walked away. He assumed that she would be thinking and doing much the same—putting the matching earring in a safe place until they had a proper moment to reconcile. Fate had other plans for them, however. The date was January 16, 1942. The plane that would have returned Carole Lombard to her home and her husband crashed into a mountainside. The couple who had loved one

Clark Gable

another so very deeply were now seemingly forever separated by her death.

Gable immediately flew to the site of the crash. He knew his soul mate was dead, but he reasoned that if he could find the other half of the pair of earrings that had been so symbolic of their final angry words to one another he would have some sense of closure on the tragedy. He never did find the piece of jewelry. Even today, no one knows just how angry Carole Lombard had been at what she saw as her husband's attempts to interfere with her plans, so no one knows what she might have done with the one remaining token of her husband's affections.

What is known is that Carole Lombard's ghost lost little time before first visiting from beyond. Lombard's

Carole Lombard

connection with the Hollywood house she began to haunt was not understood at first. The only clue to the home's specific location within Hollywood is that it was an "elegant" house in "the best part of Hollywood." Because those definitions are both highly subjective and likely to change over time, they really don't help us identify the residence in question.

The first witness to Carole Lombard's ghost was a woman named Adriana de Sola who was working as a domestic supervisor at the house. During de Sola's initial experience with the ghost she felt herself being shaken awake. After she sat up in bed and concentrated for a few moments on the strange sensation she was experiencing, an apparition appeared. The image was of a badly injured female body.

Roughly a week later, the same wraith awoke Adriana again. This time, the image was much clearer in appearance, giving the servant an opportunity to describe its appearance in detail to her employers. When she spoke of the ghostly woman's light-colored suit being covered in blood, the homeowner knew immediately that her house was haunted by the ghost of Carole Lombard. This, the owners pointed out to the frantic employee, was imminently reasonable because the late actress and Clark Gable had lived in the house for many happy years.

Adriana De Sola obviously did not think that her employment contract extended to putting up with such things as ghostly visitations; she resigned her position soon after, taking with her any way of knowing if Carole Lombard's spirit ever visited the house again. The homeowner has chosen not to publicly comment, one way or the other.

Clark Gable never fully recovered from the loss of his beloved wife. Almost immediately after her death, he volunteered for active war duty with the Army Air Corps, which he handled heroically. But from that point on, his life was little more than a series of tragedies and years of wasted potential. He remarried twice—both times to actresses who bore a strong resemblance to his beloved Carole. Not surprisingly, neither marriage was a success. It was clear that Gable was suffering dreadfully. He was drinking heavily and doing bad work in the few movie parts offered to him. Finally, in 1960, during filming of the movie *The Misfits*—a project for acclaimed director John Huston, with hot stars Marilyn Monroe and Montgomery Clift, that was planned as his comeback—

Clark Gable suffered a fatal heart attack while attempting to do a stunt sequence necessary for the picture.

Carole Lombard's soul was apparently not immediately aware of her partner's demise. During a séance held in a quiet section of Hollywood, her spirit came through after just a few minutes of silence. She seemed confused and explained that she had come back to look for the love of her life, Clark Gable. She explained that she had once found her husband, while he was still living, but he had not recognized her in her ethereal form and so she hadn't been able to apologize for her role in their parting quarrel.

Happily, according to legendary ghostly sounds emanating from the inauspicious Oatman Hotel, the two who loved one another so passionately in life likely found one another soon after Clark Gable joined Carole Lombard in the afterlife. Room 15, the one the couple rented in that small desert hostelry, is often empty now—but that hasn't stopped people from reporting the sounds of delighted whispers and satisfied giggles, intermingled with the sounds of running water coming from the room where the two spent their first nights of wedded bliss.

For the sake of Carole and Clark's perpetual happiness, and the satisfaction of romantic ghost lovers everywhere, let's hope that the sounds of toilets flushing, the sight of lights turning on and off mysteriously, and even the disembodied, phantom footsteps sounding around Room 15 are all proof that the pair are enjoying a passionate eternity.

Love This Ghost

The Hollywood Guest Inn, a small three-story hotel on Yucca Street in Hollywood once known as The Oban, has a long and haunted history. The inn served as a home away from home for many performers, including Glenn Miller, Orson Welles and Marilyn Monroe. These years of providing accommodations to up-and-coming stars seems to have earned the small hostelry several permanent residents—ghostly ones.

As with the ghosts in the Hollywood Roosevelt Hotel, the paranormal presences in this smaller hotel have created inexplicable cold spots throughout this building. Spirits of long-deceased guests still make their way up and down the stairway, perhaps coming and going from auditions, rehearsals or performances. Their continuing activity has created the pockets of cold air that are so often associated with the presence of a ghost.

The entity that hotel owner Eric Eisenberg described as a "lady ghost" haunts an area towards the front of the building's second floor. It's thought that she was the wife of a former owner who succumbed to respiratory problems. It's not known why she's chosen to haunt that one spot. It might be the area where she and her husband had their personal quarters or possibly the place where she died.

One of the ghosts in the cellar has actually allowed himself to be seen as a shadowy form. That phantom is generally believed to be the spirit of Charles Love, a stuntman and star's double. He died while staying at the hotel in February of 1933. For years it was thought that he killed

Formerly the Oban Inn, this building has been identified as being home to several ghosts.

himself while drinking, but psychics who've investigated the building wonder if his death was, in fact, a suicide. If these sensitives are correct and Love's death was either murder or an accident, that might help explain his lingering presence at the hotel—but not why the spirit remains in the cellar.

Love has a companion of sorts in his subterranean forever; there is thought to also be at least one other specter, a male, in the same area of the basement. When camera crews from Los Angeles's KTLA-TV morning news show made their way down to the basement in an attempt to film the spirits, they were met with an overwhelmingly vile odor. They tried to continue taping, and their persistence apparently paid off. Within five minutes, the air in the unventilated room became fresh-smelling once again. Perhaps the ghosts decided the publicity might be good for their new careers as ghosts.

As far as anyone knows, the presences from the past continue to coexist with those of the present in this cozy Hollywood hotel.

Act 3

HOLLYWOOD

Transported to the Great Beyond

Playbill

John Wayne (1907-1979)

The Big Trail (1930)

Stagecoach (1939)

They Were Expendable (1945)

Angel and the Badman (1947)

The Sands of Iwo Jima (1949)

The Fighting Kentuckian (1949)

She Wore a Yellow Ribbon (1949)

Rio Grande (1950)

The Quiet Man (1952)

The Alamo (1960)

*The Man Who Shot
Liberty Valance* (1962)

The Sons of Katie Elder (1965)

True Grit (1969)

Rio Lobo (1970)

Chisum (1970)

The Cowboys (1972)

The Shootist (1976)

James Dean (1931-1955)

East of Eden (1955)

Rebel Without a Cause (1955)

Giant (1956)

Errol Flynn (1909-1959)

Captain Blood (1935)

*The Charge of the
Light Brigade* (1936)

The Prince and the Pauper (1937)

The Adventures of Robin Hood (1938)

The Dawn Patrol (1938)

Dodge City (1939)

Sante Fe Trail (1940)

Virginia City (1940)

*They Died With Their
Boots On* (1941)

Gentleman Jim (1942)

The Adventures of Don Juan (1948)

*The Adventures of
Captain Fabian* (1951)

Bela Lugosi (1882-1956)	Lon Chaney, Sr. (1883-1930)
Dracula (1931)	*Treasure Island* (1920)
White Zombie (1932)	*Oliver Twist* (1922)
Island of Lost Souls (1933)	*Shadows* (1922)
The Black Cat (1934)	*The Hunchback of Notre Dame* (1923)
The Raven (1935)	
Son of Frankenstein (1939)	*The Phantom of the Opera* (1925)
The Devil Bat (1940)	*The Monster* (1925)
The Ghost of Frankenstein (1942)	*Mr. Wu* (1927)
Frankenstein Meets the Wolf Man (1943)	*London After Midnight* (1927)
	West of Zanzibar (1928)
Ghosts on the Loose (1943)	*Laugh, Clown, Laugh* (1928)
The Body Snatcher (1945)	*While the City Sleeps* (1928)
Abbott and Costello Meet Frankenstein (1948)	*The Unholy Three* (1930)
Bela Lugosi Meets a Brooklyn Gorilla (1952)	
Glen or Glenda? (1953)	
Bride of the Monster (1956)	
Plan 9 from Outer Space (1958)	

John Wayne and *The Wild Goose*

Everything about actor John Wayne was larger than life—and continued to be so long after his death. He was a completely self-made man who accomplished a great deal—and he enjoyed every one of those accomplishments and the fun that they brought him. Wayne delighted in all aspects of life, but none more than the life he could lead when he was aboard his ocean-going yacht, *The Wild Goose*.

By the spring of 1979, however, the actor's wonderful gig was almost up. At the age of 72, John Wayne was dying and he knew it. Selecting the next owner for his fabulous yacht became a heart-rending task for Wayne, a man famous for not showing his emotions. For this reason, Lynn Hutchins, a lawyer from Santa Monica, was humbled and pleased to be able to purchase the craft. Hutchins determined right from the outset that he'd keep the yacht exactly as he found it, hiring the same crew and maintaining the library and trophy wall. John Wayne died on June 11, 1979, with the assurance that his beloved yacht, *The Wild Goose*, would be well cared for.

Not long after Hutchins took possession of the vessel, he was browsing in a store that specialized in marine accessories. Suddenly and unexpectedly, he felt strongly compelled to buy a particular set of lamps. Puzzled at what he suspected was merely an uncharacteristic occurrence of impulse shopping, Lynn Hutchins returned to the yacht and hung the fixtures in place without mentioning the incident to anyone.

When a long-standing crew member saw the lamps, he was enormously surprised. They were identical to lamps that had hung in *The Wild Goose* for years, and which had only been taken down because the six-foot, four-inch John Wayne kept bumping his head into them. By coincidence, Hutchins had even hung the fixtures in exactly the same spots.

"The man's getting me to do his shopping for him," Hutchins quipped. And apparently his interior decorating as well.

The first actual ghost sighting occurred at 4:00 one morning, just outside the boat's bathroom—or "head," as it is called in nautical lingo. The image was so vivid that Hutchins thought there really was someone on board until he approached the image and watched it disappear without a trace.

Given Hutchins's description of what he had seen, it *had* to be the ghost of John Wayne. The lawyer described a "big, tall figure" that "filled the whole doorway" and wore a cowboy hat. The apparition offered "a bit of a smile" before disappearing from view. Hutchins's wife, Cynde, has also seen what she believes to be the ghost of the late actor on *The Wild Goose*. While enjoying what used to be Wayne's private shower, she sensed that someone was staring at her. The pretty young woman cut her bathing routine short and rather self-consciously got out of the cubicle with a towel in front of her. Virtually filling the doorway to the room was a large form. As she stared at the image, it vanished, taking with it her uncomfortable feeling of being watched.

John Wayne

Neither Hutchins's experience nor his wife's were on the lawyer's mind one afternoon in October of 1979 as he sat relaxing in the yacht's main salon. When he heard clinking sounds coming from the bar across the room, Hutchins got up to investigate and glanced into a mirror hanging above the bar just in time to see a tall man in cowboy attire standing directly behind the chair that Hutchins had just left. Again, the image was so sharp and solid that it fooled the boat's new owner. He thought he had a stowaway until the figure disappeared once again.

Hutchins now says that he never feels as safe anywhere as he does when he's on board *The Wild Goose*. He is certain that the former owner's spirit is a protective one and that neither man wants any harm to come to the boat. Hutchins has come to believe that the rhythmic thumping he hears on the deck every night is Wayne maintaining his habit of walking 20 laps around the ship. Given the actor's size, one wouldn't expect him to walk silently; apparently his ghost doesn't, either. Others, even those without a vested interest in *The Wild Goose*, have also reported hearing the heavy footsteps on the deck.

A dramatic incident in 1980 confirmed the ghost's protective nature. A wedding was being held on board the yacht as it rode, under its own power, among the other ships in Newport Harbor—close to the property where *The Wild Goose's* famous former owner had lived. In what was probably a simple crew error, the yacht's engines suddenly stopped without warning. The boat sat powerless in the crowded harbor. Without the engines functioning, there was no way to control the ship; an uncontrolled ship in an enclosed and crowded body of water was an accident waiting to happen. Worse, it takes several minutes to restart the engines once they go dead.

To the complete amazement of all those aboard, *The Wild Goose* did not float about aimlessly while the crew was working to return the ship's power—far from it! Instead, the yacht moved in a controlled manner—against the force of a 40-knot wind—and came to rest gently in the soft mud at the shore in front of John Wayne's former home. It doesn't take much of a stretch of the imagination to conclude that the craft's previous owner had taken over the controls during the emergency.

After Lynn Hutchins had owned the yacht for a number

of years and was completely comfortable with the actor's continuing ghostly presence, he invited a group of psychics on board the 140-foot yacht. After exploring the craft, they brought back even more information than Hutchins had expected. One member of the group, Janice Hayes, reported receiving strongly negative vibrations while in the crew area below deck. She determined that there had been controversy surrounding a young crew member who'd shown too much of an independent streak for his own good.

The ship's records confirmed her feelings; 20 years earlier, two young deckhands and a third young man defied direct orders by taking a small boat out while *The Wild Goose* was anchored in choppy waters. The trip proved to be just as dangerous as had been anticipated and resulted in both crew members drowning.

Hutchins was certainly not surprised when the group identified the hallway leading to the head as a "hot spot," because this was where he had first encountered the actor's ghostly manifestation. One of the psychic investigators even reported receiving an expression of love from John Wayne for his longtime friend Patricia Stacey.

The psychics also determined that the boat was still home to a former crew member, probably a man named Peter Stein. Stein served as captain of the ship until his death in 1969 and was a stereotypically colorful sort of old salt whose company John Wayne had always thoroughly enjoyed.

Because these presences have always given the impression of benevolence, it is easy to see why *The Wild Goose's* owner, Lynn Hutchins, feels very much at home aboard his enormous haunted yacht.

James Dean's Possessed Porsche

Cursed. Haunted. As the following strange and tragic paranormal story illustrates, these two words might occasionally be considered synonyms.

On the last day of September 1955, just as Friday afternoon was becoming Friday evening, 24-year-old Donald Gene Turnupseed steered his black and white, late-model Ford eastbound along California's Route 466. It was 5:57 PM, and nothing indicated that the college student's trip home to Tulare for the weekend would be anything but routine. Until he prepared to turn left onto the northbound lanes of State Highway 41, Donald had no way of knowing that his future was about to be tragically and irrevocably changed.

Along the westbound lane of the same stretch of road, Rolf Wuetherich, a mechanic just a few years older than Donald, reached around to the back seat of the silver Porsche Spyder in which he was a passenger. Wuetherich grabbed a jacket that had been thrown there by the Porsche's owner, who was quite intent on driving. The driver's concentrated focus was understandable given that later calculations indicated he was driving at speeds in excess of 85 miles per hour.

Completely unaware of one another's existence, the two vehicles continued on their collision course to disaster. Seconds later, the Ford was a crumbled heap, the Porsche nearly ripped in two. Donald Turnupseed, his head badly cut, lay prone across the black and white car's seat. The impact of the nearly head-on crash threw Rolf Wuetherich 20 feet. When he landed, his jaw was fractured, one of his legs was broken and many of his internal organs were damaged. On the seat of what was left of the silver gray Porsche Spyder, the driver, James Dean, lay lifeless.

The sudden death of the 24-year-old movie actor, a major star in the making, instantly created a full-blown legend. Word of the fatal accident spread quickly throughout the motion picture industry and, as it did, an eerie story began to unfold. Dean, who loved cars, had only owned the Spyder for a few weeks. With great affection, he named the car "Little Bastard." As fond as he was of the luxurious automobile, his friends were leery of it. Many of them had warned him to be extra careful while driving the car. Actress Ursula Andress told Dean in no uncertain terms that the car gave her a bad feeling. British actor Alec Guiness had also sensed danger and advised the young star, "If you're smart, you'll get rid of that car."

When fellow actor Nick Adams also offered a negative opinion of the vehicle, Dean confided to him that all such warnings were futile. Apparently James Dean had a premonitory conviction that it was his destiny to die in a speeding car. During a television interview after the filming of *Rebel Without a Cause*, the show's host prompted Dean to encourage young people to drive carefully. Dean's words were, in all likelihood, meant to be flippant but were meaningful in retrospect. The actor advised youngsters behind the wheel to slow down because "the life you save could be mine." Ironically, Dean had received a speeding

James Dean

ticket just two hours before his fatal collision, but he failed to heed *that* warning, too.

Undeniably, actors belong to a unique community—a family of sorts. Their lives are, in many ways, very different from those of the rest of the population. For one thing, they must be much more in touch with emotions than the rest of us need to be—after all, tapping into emotions is the actor's meal ticket. This heightened sensitivity, combined with the acting community's feeling of kinship for its members, might explain the large number of warnings Dean had received. Some explanation is necessary, considering that those who were advising Dean had no particular interest in or knowledge of cars.

George Barris, however, was different. He was not an actor but an experienced automotive designer who had worked on James Dean's other cars. Despite his objective and knowledgeable background, Barris declared that, from the first moment he laid eyes on the Porsche Spyder, he felt that it gave off "a weird feeling of impending doom."

Whatever malevolent force those people were sensing seemed only to become stronger after the car had succeeded in killing James Dean.

The Spyder was beyond repair after the accident, but George Barris recognized that the pricey Porsche parts could be useful. With that in mind, he bought the wreck from the insurance company and had it shipped to his place of business. As the mangled remains of the car were being unloaded from the delivery truck, the wreckage toppled over and landed on one of Barris's employees, breaking the man's leg.

Two physicians, Dr. Troy McHenry and Dr. William Eschrid, were the next to suffer the wrath of the seemingly possessed car. The men were both car racing enthusiasts. McHenry bought the Porsche's engine, while Eschrid bought its drive-train. Both men installed the parts from Dean's ill-fated auto into vehicles they were intending to race on October 24 of the following year. During the competition, McHenry mysteriously lost control of his car. It barreled full-speed into a tree and Dr. Troy McHenry died instantly.

Eschrid was, by comparison, more fortunate. He lived through the horrible collision that *he* was involved in that day, but later reported that, for reasons he couldn't explain, he had simply lost control of his car.

Back at Barris's garage, not realizing the potentially serious act he was committing, a youngster tried to steal the wrecked Porsche's steering wheel. This clandestine souvenir hunting was obviously a bad plan for both that fan and the one who tried to cut out a piece of blood-stained seat upholstery as a gruesome souvenir. The pair of would-be thieves were both badly injured during their attempts to make off with the parts.

Another man bought the Spyder's two undamaged tires and later told Barris that both had blown out simultaneously. At that point, the car designer had had enough. He put what remained of the destroyed automobile in storage, but even that did not stop the carnage. The Porsche's deadly agenda was actually becoming more aggressive.

When the California Highway Patrol approached George Barris about displaying the destroyed vehicle to young drivers as a means of stressing the importance of safe driving, Barris was delighted. Finally, he thought, the car—and whatever had haunted or hexed it—could potentially save lives.

And, for the first two stops on the police tour, it looked as though Barris had been correct. It wasn't until the evening after the third show that the car's spirit turned vicious again. For reasons that have never been satisfactorily explained, the garage where the wreck was being held overnight burst into flames. The building burned to the ground, as did the one next door. All of the cars in the garage were completely consumed by the raging inferno— all but one. Scorched paint was the only damage to the Porsche Spyder.

The next stop on the police safety tour was Sacramento. There, the Porsche fell from its display platform, badly injuring a teenage boy who had been standing beside the twisted, scorched frame of the car. The Spyder was then loaded onto a flatbed truck and sent toward its next destination— Salinas, the city that had been James Dean's destination on the day his fatal accident occurred. The Porsche's second trip to Salinas also ended in death; the truck driver lost control of the huge vehicle and was thrown from the cab. The Porsche, which had torn away from its tethers, broke loose and fell on the man, killing him instantly.

What remained of the Little Bastard's specter was inactive for the next few months, but in 1958 the parking brake on a truck that was transporting the car failed. The truck rolled into a store window. Miraculously, considering both the amount of damage done and the car's history, no one was injured.

The last time James Dean's infamous car was on public display, it simply shattered. Although no one was touching it at the time, what had been left of the once-valuable car cracked into 11 parts. No one was injured in that mishap either, so the evil presence may have been weakening, perhaps because it had begun to spread beyond the car itself and onto the people associated with James Dean and his "Little Bastard."

Nick Adams, Dean's long-time friend and confidante, had reluctantly accepted a producer's offer to serve as a stand-in for James Dean so that the late actor's final scenes in the movie *Giant* could be completed. It was the last role Adams ever played; in 1968, he died of a strange and unexpected drug overdose. Lance Reventlow, who had first recommended that Dean purchase the Porsche Spyder, was killed in a plane crash. Sal Mineo, Dean's friend and co-star in *Rebel Without a Cause*, was stabbed to death. Natalie Wood, the female lead in *Rebel*, drowned in a controversial boating accident. Rolf Wuetherich, Dean's passenger at the time of the lethal collision, was sentenced to life in prison after being convicted of murdering his wife.

But, what of the haunted (or cursed) Porsche Spyder itself? Unfortunately, I cannot tell you. No one can. En route to a safety display in Miami, the car disappeared. Not even a part of the Little Bastard has ever been seen since.

Although we have no way of knowing whether the car was possessed before Dean bought it or if something in the actor's destiny managed to set the wheels of tragedy in motion, research indicates that, as extraordinary as this tale is, it is not an isolated incident. Other cases of haunted or possessed cars (not counting Stephen King's fictional account in the novel *Christine*) can be found throughout history.

Many believe the limousine that was carrying Austrian Archduke Ferdinand when he was assassinated on June 28,

1914, was cursed. The bullet that killed him became known as "the shot that was heard around the world" because it precipitated World War I. Tallying war casualties, a case could be made for that car having been indirectly involved in causing some 8,000,000 deaths.

While that connection may be a stretch, the fact that the car was later directly linked to at least 18 bizarre, sudden and premature deaths does beg comparisons to James Dean's Porsche Spyder.

After the Archduke's death, the car was used by a general in the Austrian Army whose career had been a stellar one up to that time. Shortly after the general began using the vehicle, he was inexplicably relieved of his duties. He lived the rest of his life in poverty and died in an insane asylum. A captain who had served under that general took over the car next. One week later, he and two pedestrians died in a freak collision between the car and a cart. Once the car was repaired, the Government of Yugoslavia took it over as a limousine for a high-ranking governor; he endured a series of increasingly serious "accidents" while riding in the car and finally ordered it demolished. The tragic tale might have ended there, but greed took over in the form of a Doctor Srkis, who bought the car for its value as scrap metal and then rebuilt it. Six months later, when Srkis was alone in the vehicle, it overturned on a straight stretch of road. Strangely, the doctor was killed but the car was not damaged and, as part of the doctor's estate, it was soon back on the market. The jeweler who purchased the auto unexpectedly killed himself less than a year later. The next owner only lived a week after taking over the car. In an amazing similarity to the James Dean case, the evil car's next owner entered it in a race during which he failed to negotiate a curve, with fatal consequences. Again the car was sold for scrap, and again the new owner died just days after buying it. A man who thought he could turn a fast profit bought the mangled heap, rebuilt and repainted the car, and offered it for sale once again. When no one stepped forward to buy it, he decided to become a part-time chauffeur and use the car as a limousine. While driving a wedding party of six to the church, he lost control of the car and everyone riding in the car was killed. After that the car—and apparently the curse—was put to rest.

Tasmanian Devil

On Monday, December 18, 1978, an Anglican archdeacon, a Catholic priest, a boat painter and a handful of others gathered around a two-and-a-half foot long model of an ocean-going yacht sometimes known as *Zaca* and sometimes known as *The Black Witch*. The little group had assembled to perform an exorcism. They wanted to free the ship of the ghost that had been haunting it for nearly 20 years—the ghost of actor Errol Flynn.

While Flynn was for a time a popular and successful actor, his personal life was far from exemplary. The man who played swashbuckling heroes on the silver screen was cowardly, had disrespectful manners, questionable ethics and distasteful moral standards. In the role of decent human being, Errol Flynn was unconvincing to say the least. He loved to party, preferably with as many young women as possible. His favorite party place was aboard his yacht, which he had named *Zaca*, a Samoan word meaning peace.

It was undoubtedly the consequences of Errol Flynn's debauched lifestyle that led to his financial and physical ruin. On October 14, 1959, Flynn collapsed while partying aboard the *Zaca* in Vancouver, British Columbia. The other partiers, including his 16-year-old female companion, rushed him to a hospital. It was too late. He had suffered a massive heart attack. Errol Flynn was 50 years old, almost penniless and quite suddenly dead.

Flynn's once-promising life had begun in Tasmania, but it ended in disgrace in the Canadian coastal city. Once a popular character, Flynn had alienated most of his peers by the time of his death. Although his funeral was held at Hollywood's Forest Lawn Cemetery, it was poorly attended and the actor was laid to rest in an initially unmarked grave. Despite this lack of veneration, it wasn't too long before Errol Flynn evidently began to enjoy his afterlife.

Meanwhile, the *Zaca* was sold to a couple with ambitious sailing plans. Their initial voyage to Europe went well, but when they tried to return, the craft broke down. At great danger and expense to themselves, the new owners had the vessel towed to a shipyard on the French Riviera, where they simply abandoned her. For many years, the boat on which Errol Flynn had once partied with some of Hollywood's most glamorous people was left to disintegrate.

Dock workers soon became aware that the *Zaca* was not decaying peacefully. In some strange way that they neither liked nor understood, security guards and other witnesses could see signs of life aboard the forsaken yacht. Once night had fallen in the shipyard, the ghost of Errol Flynn was frequently recognized pacing along the deck of the *Zaca*. A guard who went to investigate the apparition was so frightened by what he'd seen that he jumped into the frigid water below. When rescued, he was incoherent with fear.

The skipper of a yacht stored in an adjoining slip reported listening to the distinct sounds of a party coming from the *Zaca* one night. "It was a wild party," the man claimed. "Girls' voices … laughter … lights were going on and off." Despite all he heard and saw, the man acknowledged that "there couldn't have been a party … no one was aboard—there wasn't even electricity." Still," the man conceded, "something strange was going on."

By December of 1978, the shipyard's owners must have had enough of the unsettling reports associated with their place of business. After commissioning a model builder to construct a small replica of the *Zaca*, they arranged for an exorcism to be conducted in Monte Carlo.

The ritual was performed according to standard protocol for such ceremonies. During the exorcism, the painter moaned and then lost consciousness for a few moments in an apparent faint. Some theorize that he was, for that moment, possessed by the spirit of Errol Flynn as the actor finally left this world for the next.

Whether or not the exorcism was a success, it is doubtful that any incarnation of the *Zaca* continues to ply the waters of the world. Errol Flynn's revenant, however, visits the Haunted Houses chapter of this book (see p. 51).

Poignant Pioneers

As stars in some of the film industry's earliest horror movies, Bela Lugosi and Lon Chaney were among the first actors to entertain their audiences by frightening them. Chaney was to have played the lead role in the movie *Dracula*, but he died before production of the classic even began. As a result, Hungarian stage actor Lugosi was cast as the evil vampire. It was a part Bela Lugosi loved so much that, in making arrangements for his own funeral, he requested that his remains be cloaked in the character's dramatic black cape. In life, both actors loved not only the glamour and glitter of show business but Hollywood itself. In death, they both haunted Tinseltown.

Lon Chaney was a dandy. Whether his luck was running hot or cold, the actor dressed immaculately. He always took public transportation and began every sojourn dressed to the nines, proudly sitting on the bus bench at Hollywood and Vine. When he was working, the bus on that route would take Chaney to the studio. When he wasn't working, Chaney's destination was less clear but his routine was unchanged. He simply loved that intersection, what it represented, and the fact that he was a part of that representation.

For many years after his death, Chaney's image, still straight and proud, could be seen sitting on the bus bench at Hollywood and Vine. After the bench was removed, the actor's image was no longer seen. Perhaps by now his own personal bus to eternity has arrived to take him to a place where his sense of the dramatic is appreciated more consistently than it was on earth.

Bela Lugosi

Like Lon Chaney, a nattily dressed Bela Lugosi would stride along Hollywood Boulevard—even when he was too poor to feed himself. And, like his counterpart, he carried this tradition with him to the grave and beyond.

As the result of an agreement between local funeral home operators and the owners of the retail outlets along Hollywood Boulevard, no funeral processions ever wind their way along that street. The retailers on the strip don't want anything as negative as the reality of death to impose itself on their customers' moods. Anyone whose job entails driving a hearse in Hollywood is familiar with alternative routes to and from churches, cemeteries and funeral homes.

In 1959, the man driving the car carrying Lugosi's remains was no exception. Yet, en route to the cemetery, the hearse suddenly turned a corner and proceeded along the actor's favorite stretch of Hollywood Boulevard. Badly shaken by the incident, the driver later said that the hearse seemed to be beyond his control—just for that one block.

Upon hearing of the procession's strange detour, those who knew Bela Lugosi and his beloved walk simply smiled. They were sure that the man's sense of the dramatic had dictated one last "goodbye" to the area he had loved so dearly.

That final act seems to have satisfied Lugosi's spirit; although the run-down Hollywood apartment building where he lived and died is definitely haunted, the resident ghost is that of a dreadfully unhappy woman. Tenants report that she can be a bit of a nuisance when she moves their furniture and causes small items to disappear. But, for the most part, the ghost is accepted with great compassion because she is most often heard sobbing piteously.

Act **4**

HOLLYWOOD

Ghosts in Public

Playbill

Marilyn Monroe (1926-1962)

Monkey Business (1952)

How to Marry a Millionaire (1953)

Niagara (1953)

Gentlemen Prefer Blondes (1953)

The Seven Year Itch (1955)

Bus Stop (1956)

The Prince and the Showgirl (1957)

The Asphalt Jungle (1957)

Some Like It Hot (1959)

The Misfits (1961)

Peg Entwistle (1908-1932)

Thirteen Women (1932)

Lionel Barrymore (1878–1954)

Mata Hari (1931)

Rasputin and the Empress (1932)

Grand Hotel (1932)

Dinner at Eight (1933)

Treasure Island (1934)

David Copperfield (1935)

Captains Courageous (1937)

Young Dr. Kildare (1938)

It's a Wonderful Life (1946)

Duel in the Sun (1946)

Key Largo (1948)

Ethel Barrymore (1879–1959)

The Final Judgment (1915)

Rasputin and the Empress (1932)

None But the Lonely Heart (1944)

The Farmer's Daughter (1947)

The Paradine Case (1947)

Deadline USA (1952)

Young At Heart (1955)

Griffith Park Phantoms

At the northeast corner of Hollywood, nestled in the eastern Santa Monica Mountain range, lies the spectacular Griffith Park. At just less than 4100 acres, this is the largest municipal park and urban wilderness area in the United States. By way of comparison, New York City's Central Park has just 843 acres. The beautifully maintained public resource includes a world-class observatory, the Autry Museum of Western History, the legendary Greek Theatre, the L.A. Zoo, a still-functioning 1926-era merry-go-round, an equestrian center and a miniature railroad—but a huge portion of the park is still wilderness.

Making your way to the highest point of the park's 1640-foot elevation can pose a challenge whether you're on foot, horseback or bicycle. Of course, driving up Mount Hollywood is easy, but then the challenge becomes finding a place to leave your car in this popular getaway spot. Once you get to the top, the 360-degree view makes it all worthwhile. As you stand at this amazing pinnacle, you can look down at the Los Angeles Basin, the San Fernando Valley, the San Gabriel Mountains, Catalina Island and, mostly importantly for our purposes, the famous (and haunted) Hollywood sign. You see, Griffith Park not only has a long and important connection with the movie industry, it also has an even older ghost story.

* * *

In the early days of movie making, producers with an eye to saving money decided that it was unnecessary to go to the expense of shooting a film at a specific distant location. One producer is said to have declared, "A tree is a tree and a rock is a rock." Because there were plenty of both in nearby beautiful Griffith Park, that philosophy and the economics behind it caught on. As a result, portions of many movies, including *The Terminator*, *Jurassic Park* and *The Rocketeer*, have been filmed there.

Budget constraints were not the reason that Warner Brothers chose Griffith Park as the locale for several pivotal scenes in the 1955 film *Rebel Without a Cause*. In that movie, the park was not merely used as the disguised backdrop of an undisclosed location—the Griffith Park Observatory and the grounds surrounding it were dramatically cast and proudly identified.

A long-standing legend indicates that, in addition to those movies, a very different film could also be made on the land that is now known as Griffith Park. And that film would not be a work of fiction but a documentary of a true ghost story.

Originally part of a Spanish land grant called Rancho Los Feliz, the land was privately owned by the 1800s. In the middle of that century, a man named Leon Baldwin bought the spread from a lawyer's estate. Over his years of business dealings, Baldwin had earned himself the nickname, "Lucky." That moniker was soon to have a sadly ironic ring to it. According to an unofficial historian named Major Horace Bell, the ranch into which Baldwin put so much effort, enthusiasm and expertise collapsed around him. According to Bell, "The cattle sickened and died in the fields. The dairy business was a disastrous failure. Fire destroyed the ripening grain and … grasshoppers devoured the green crops. The vineyard was struck with a strange blight and perished."

Eventually, the man once known as "Lucky" was forced to walk away from the ranch, barely managing to cover the balance remaining on the mortgage. Baldwin must have been devastated by the loss. If only he'd known the history of the land he'd bought, he might have understood. Then again, he might not have bought the land in the first place if he had realized that it was cursed.

Don Antonio Feliz, the man whose family had first developed the property, contracted a deadly case of smallpox. When it was clear that Feliz only had hours to live, two unscrupulous men came to visit him. They drew up a will for Feliz indicating that he wished to leave the enormous spread of land to them. Feliz was too weak to protest, and after the man's death this coerced will was ruled to be legal and binding.

Don Antonio's niece, Petranilla, was furious at this turn of events. When she was not able to win her point in court she resorted to another tactic—she laid a curse on the men and the stolen land. The potential power of that curse was probably what motivated the swindlers to immediately turn the ranch over to a lawyer. The lawyer appears to have been naïve and greedy enough to be delighted with the gift. One of his first challenges was to assure that there would be a sufficient supply of water to the land. He worked long and hard toward that end, but he was shot and killed while celebrating his success in making the necessary arrangements.

Colonel Griffith Jenkins Griffith, for whom the park is now named, became the next owner. The powerful curse apparently continued to plague the land even then. During a vicious storm, rain fell in torrents and lightning struck one old oak tree after another. Several of Griffith's ranch hands who were watching the storm maintained that, as the bolts of lightning illuminated the area, they saw a gruesome-looking skeletal figure dancing just above the ground throughout the entire storm.

When the deluge subsided, Griffith ordered his workers to begin cleaning up. The ghostly skeleton made a point to silently stand over the men as they sawed oak branches into firewood and cleared paths of debris. It's probably safe to assume that the men worked as quickly as possible in order to escape the watchful presence of their overseer from beyond.

Griffith himself was a bizarre character whose increasingly erratic and dangerous behavior may have been caused by the curse on his land. Born in Glamorganshire, South Wales, Griffith immigrated to the United States in 1865. After kicking around as a newspaperman, he eventually made a huge personal fortune in gold mine speculation. Part of this fortune was used to buy the enormous Rancho Los Feliz in 1882. Griffith sold some of the ranch's water rights to the city two years later, recouping most of his investment.

Colonel Griffith was something of a diminutive peacock. He was often seen strutting around town in his trademark outfit of a long cream-colored overcoat and a gold-headed cane. The colonel (no record of military service exists, and most historians assume that Griffith bestowed this title on himself in order to sound more important) wasn't exactly known for his winning personality. One acquaintance described Griffith as "a midget egomaniac." Another said that the colonel was "a roly-poly, pompous little fellow" who "had an exaggerated strut like a turkey gobbler."

In 1903, Griffith's already eccentric demeanor took a dramatic turn for the worse. He was constantly nervous and edgy and bit his fingernails down to the quick. His lawyer claimed that Griffith had also begun "sneak drinking"—guzzling as much as two quarts of whiskey a day in private while outwardly aligning himself with the city's temperance movement.

In August, Griffith and his wife checked into the Arcadia Hotel in Santa Monica. Christina Griffith hoped that a holiday would help her husband to relax, but his strange behavior only increased. On the last day of the Griffiths' vacation, Christina was gathering her belongings when her husband entered the room with a handgun. Christina was shot in the head, but she survived by throwing herself out a window and crawling to safety. The shooting left Christina Griffith disfigured and blind in one eye.

At the Colonel's trial, his attorneys argued that heavy drinking had caused Griffith to suffer from "alcoholic insanity." Astonishingly, this defense worked and the colonel was sentenced to just two years in prison.

While at San Quentin, the colonel refused both special treatment and a chance at parole. He served his full sentence, during which time his agitation and peculiar nervous tics seemed to disappear completely.

Colonel Griffith J. Griffith never again lived on his property at Rancho Los Feliz. After his release from prison, the colonel made a gift of the land to the City of Los Angeles. Was Griffith trying to buy his way back into public favor? Was he truly contrite and eager to give something back to the city that had made him so wealthy? Or was Griffith convinced that his weird murderous delusions had been caused by an evil entity on the cursed ranch property? We will probably never know for certain.

The identity of the soul haunting the property did not become known until after Griffith donated the land to the city for use as a public park. City administrators had assembled to celebrate Griffith's gift. Ironically, they chose to hold their celebration in the old adobe building where Don Antonio Feliz had both lived and died. At midnight, when the celebrants were at their most jubilant, a "fleshless face" appeared over the table at which the men had been sitting. "Señors, I am Antonio Feliz," the specter announced. "I have come to invite you to dine with me in hell."

Presumably, the supernatural party-crasher caused a sudden end to the festive meeting. Although he has not been seen or sensed since, Don Antonio Feliz's ghost is still occasionally blamed if something goes wrong around the park. That bit of scapegoating aside, the endowment of the land for public use seems to have laid the curse, and therefore Feliz's restless spirit, to rest.

Animated Afterlife

Located southeast of Hollywood in Anaheim, Disneyland is to animated film stars what Hollywood is to flesh-and-blood ones. The theme park is home to a legion of artificially created movie legends. Yes, they're cartoon characters, but they're also stars. Why, Mickey Mouse even played a leading role in the Academy Award-winning movie *Fantasia*. Just like their real-life counterparts, cartoon characters apparently have to audition for the different roles they might like to play and, in this instance, Mickey's famous role as the sorcerer's apprentice nearly went to Dopey of the Seven Dwarfs. Only a last-minute decision by Walt Disney, the creator of both of the animated characters, ensured that generations of movie-goers have delighted in watching Mickey Mouse struggle to keep up with the sorcerer's magical demands. If any of Mickey's fans from *Fantasia* ever miss the delightful little mouse, they can always find him at Disneyland among the rides and other featured attractions.

But Mickey Mouse isn't the only slightly unusual entity that visitors to the famous theme park might encounter; there are ghost stories associated with Disneyland, just as there are with Hollywood. It must be admitted, however, that the well-circulated amusement park tales could be what are known as "urban legends." These twice-told (at least!) tales are now part of California folklore. They may be all but impossible to verify, but that lack of substantiation certainly doesn't diminish their entertainment value.

First, of course, we must dismiss certain ghostly residents of Disneyland—those found in the attraction known as the Haunted Mansion. Such ghosts are certainly not ethereal beings but mechanically generated components of that particular venue. Or perhaps we shouldn't be too quick in dismissing *all* of the ghosts in the Haunted Mansion as having been artificially created. Even Walt Disney once made a comment which seemed to imply that he thought the house might actually be haunted. As Disney himself can now only be available to us in ghostly form, we have no way of verifying his seriousness when he made that statement.

There *are*, however, said to be ghosts in the amusement park that are in no way connected to the Haunted Mansion. One of the most frequently repeated paranormal stories from Disneyland involves a conveyance known as the People Mover. Once a proud part of Tomorrowland, the ride represented a theoretical futuristic form of mass transportation. The attraction no longer exists; if the ghost of the People Mover is still active, it is probably miles away from Disneyland, perhaps haunting a pile of scrap metal.

The origin of this tale is a tragic one. A teenage boy, apparently part of a class celebrating graduation from high school, either accidentally fell, was pushed, or jumped from the People Mover. In the seconds before his body was dragged under the rapidly moving mechanism, he reached up to grab onto something with which he could pull himself to safety. The only purchase his hand found was a lock of his girlfriend's hair, which, of course, soon slid from his grasp. Seconds later, he was pulled under and to his death.

After that incident, many young women, especially those with hair similar to that of the dead boy's girlfriend, reported feeling phantom tugs on their long locks as they rode the People Mover. Most who experienced the ghostly pulls assumed that the annoying sensation was caused by the ghost of the boy who had died. Even in death, they reasoned, he was continuing to try to save himself in the way that had failed him the first time.

In a plot eerily similar to that of the Disney company's computer-animated hit *Toy Story*, the animatronic dolls at the "It's a Small World" ride have been seen moving about long after the venue has been closed for the day and the power to the attraction has been turned off. This attraction was not original to Disneyland but came to the park after a successful run in New York City as a UNICEF exhibit at the 1964 World's Fair. Originally accompanied by a musical show with actors posing as dolls from many different lands, the exhibit was enormously popular and deemed to be worth not only preserving in permanent form but transporting clear across the country in order to delight future generations. Mechanical "doll actors"—consisting of 436 animated human figures and 169 animal figures—replaced all of the flesh-and-blood cast when "It's a Small World" moved to Anaheim, but legend has it that three of the original actors in the old musical show have stayed on—in spirit anyway— and that their specters create a ghostly late-night show.

Probably the best known ghost legend from Disneyland is the one connected with the ride called the Matterhorn

Bobsleds. A woman named Dolly had been enjoying the ride with children who were seated in the sleigh-like contraption behind her. Concerned about their well-being, Dolly undid her seat belt, stood up and turned around to check on them. Just as she did, the ride went into a sudden descent and, because she was not seated and belted in, Dolly was thrown to her death. Rumor has it that the impact killed the woman instantly. The portion of the Matterhorn track where this happened has come to be called "Dolly's Dip." For understandable reasons, many believe that the mother's spirit has haunted the ride ever since.

In another area of the park, a trio of ghostly shapes has frequently been reported on Tom Sawyer's Island. Employees responsible for closing down that area at the end of the business day have reportedly seen images of boys on the outcropping of land. Because ensuring the security of the park is part of their job description, those workers have to make their way across the "river" to search the place, presuming they're going to find a trio of tourists that have somehow been left behind. But every time they come away empty handed. Those who believe that the shadowy figures are ghosts also believe that they are the spirits of three youngsters who drowned in the artificial river and that their souls have now taken refuge on the island. Some say it is unlikely that three boys could have drowned in water that never exceeds five feet in depth, but to those who have seen the apparitions, those supernatural presences are very real.

In case you think that the haunting of Disneyland is a unique occurrence, you might be interested to learn that there is at least one more haunted amusement park in California, another one in Ohio, and two that are known of in Canada. It seems that no matter what your definition of "amusing" might be, these theme parks are definite attractions—for both the living and the dead.

Time and Again

Many people have reported experiencing retrocognition when standing near this sign—they see and hear noises from a house, once occupied by the notorious Charles Manson "family," that was demolished years ago.

The experience of seeing or sensing the past is defined as retrocognition. This fascinating phenomena is thought to be the result of a person's temporary displacement in time. When such a shift occurs, it creates an opportunity to review or experience historical events. Some paranormal

At this seemingly ordinary intersection, witnesses have reported seeing vivid scenes from long ago that involve a horse-drawn stagecoach. These historic visions fade away before the viewer can appreciate that he or she has just experienced the supernatural phenomenon known as retrocognition.

investigators have speculated that retrocognition occurs more frequently than we recognize because such fleeting temporal dislocation can easily be written off as a figment of the witness's imagination. Two extremely dramatic examples of this strange paranormal oddity are associated with Hollywood.

The entrance to Runyon Park is called The Pines. Not far away, one of the world's most infamous houses stood for many years. The once breathtaking estate, however, was demolished after it had served as the home base of the Charles Manson "family." For years now, only ruins of the building's foundations have existed. Despite this, people in neighboring properties have reported seeing the old house and hearing party sounds emanating from it. Psychics who tried to investigate the apparition were warned by a disembodied, malevolent voice to "get out."

Charles Manson

Just a few blocks away, at the intersection of Sierra Bonita and Hollywood Boulevard, there is a much older example of retrocognition. This scene dates back to the days of the horse-drawn stagecoach. Modern-day motorists and pedestrians who have seen the phenomenon report that the images of the old coach are so solid and realistic that the witnesses initially assumed they'd happened upon location filming for a movie. When the scene before their eyes disappeared as quickly as it had appeared, they knew that they'd encountered something far more unusual than merely the work of a production crew. In fact, one driver was so startled by what he saw before him that he drove off the road and hit a tree.

Marilyn Gets Around

Marilyn Monroe's ghost seems to be reaching out across time to appear in many different venues. The gorgeous blonde's spirit has been busy since the death of her physical body in August of 1962. A review of Monroe's career is all but unnecessary because she is at least as famous now as she was when she was alive. Marilyn's work in movies and her extraordinary sensuality have perpetuated, and even increased, the screen idol's fame since her death—a death which, in hindsight, may have been caused by her own misadventure.

The first person visited by the spirit of Marilyn Monroe was Kenny Kingston, a man often referred to as "the psychic to the stars." It was not surprising that Monroe's ghost would choose Kingston to contact; she had relied on his sensitivity for guidance during her lifetime. Since that first materialization, her spirit has manifested itself to many others, often with the same desire—to let others know that she killed herself accidentally.

That claim—which sounds strange considering she died of a medication overdose and banal in contrast to conspiracy theorists' wishes to link her death with either the Kennedy clan or the Mafia—can actually be justified. Marilyn Monroe was a very troubled individual. In an attempt to buffer her pain, she had turned to pills. She soon became thoroughly addicted to many prescription substances, including sleeping pills. Her spirit claims to have

Marilyn Monroe

had no intention of killing her physical body that night. Apparently she only wanted to temporarily escape into the respite that sleep would bring. Unfortunately, after so many years of reliance on the drugs, her tolerance for them had increased to the point where she needed more and more of the medication in order for it to be effective. This was why, on the night of her death, Marilyn Monroe had taken one pill after another until she had unwittingly reached a lethal dose.

Since then, the movie star's revenant has consistently put a great deal of effort into trying to set the record straight. The most remarkable feat credited to her ghost was appearing in a photograph holding a sheet of paper on which the words "Mistake—Not Suicide" were typed.

Her image has also been seen at the Hollywood Roosevelt Hotel. A large mirror, which once hung in a room that Marilyn frequently rented in the hotel, has been moved to the basement elevator foyer. Observers have reported seeing Monroe's glamorous image reflected in the glass.

Rumor has it that Marilyn's love of the camera did not die with her. Fans wanting only to photograph the gorgeous star's final resting place at Westwood Memorial Park have occasionally come away with an extra image on a shot or two. Those who have seen these anomalous pictures say the additional presence strongly resembles Marilyn Monroe.

During a séance, Monroe informed the participants that her soul would be reborn in 1980. Given the dreadful unhappiness that beauty and fame brought the soul when it was incarnated as Marilyn Monroe, and its restlessness after that body's death, we can only hope her spirit now lives in joyful obscurity.

Haunted Landmark

"H-O-L-L-Y-W-O-O-D"—the larger-than-life sign on Mount Lee in the Hollywood Hills is a reflection of the community it identifies. Both the sign and the community are distinct, conspicuous and recognized by people around the world. They are also both very haunted.

The famous Hollywood landmark, which in its original incarnation spelled out "Hollywoodland," the name of a planned subdivision, was intended only as a temporary installation. In 1923, when the area we know today as Hollywood was being developed, a man named John. D. Roche was commissioned to build the 50' by 30' letters and erect them in the Hollywood Hills to advertise the new housing development. Mules and laborers hauled telegraph poles up the slope, where they were hammered and arranged to spell out the desired word. Then, on the off-chance that someone might miss seeing the enormous letters (which could, of course, be seen for many miles), a final subtle touch was added—a mere 4000 light bulbs.

Even Roche expected that, once the landmark had attracted the number of home buyers needed to make the real estate venture profitable, the advertisement would be dismantled. His prediction couldn't have been less accurate, and those "temporary" letters stood in varying states of decay and disrepair for many years. In 1949, when a change was finally made, it was only to remove the suffix "land." By then, the sign had become as permanent and prominent a feature on the local landscape as Hollywood itself had become to the world's entertainment landscape. In 1973, the sign was officially declared a local monument by the Cultural Heritage Board of the City of Los Angeles. In 1978 the old sign was retired and replaced with one made of durable steel letters and costing nearly a quarter of a millions dollars. Donors, may of them celebrities, contributed $27,700 each to buy a replacement letter. The new sign was unveiled live on Hollywood's 75th anniversary on November 14, 1978, before a television audience of 60 million.

To many people, those huge letters absolutely symbolize show business itself. This was certainly the case for young Lillian Millicent "Peg" Entwistle. From the time she was 17 years old, Peg had tried to forge a career for herself as an actress. In 1931, at the age of 23, she left New York, where she had been an active member of the Theater Guild, and moved west to try her luck with the movie industry. Peg wasn't really risking much by leaving. All she had amassed for her efforts so far was a résumé of eight straight stage flops.

When, a year later, Peg was cast in the RKO Studios production of *Thirteen Women*, it looked as though her move to Hollywood had paid off. Peg's elation, however, was agonizingly short-lived. The movie previewed to poor reviews in Santa Monica on August 20, 1932. Worse, very little of Entwistle's role had survived the cutting room. Despite this, by the time the production premiered on October 14, 1932, the devastated actress had succeeded in making herself a Hollywood legend. The fame and recognition she failed to attract in life had finally come—in death.

On Sunday, September 18, 1932, on a pleasant but otherwise unremarkable Southern California evening, 24-year-old Peg Entwistle climbed the Hollywood Hills toward the gigantic letters of the "Hollywoodland" sign. After leaving her handbag, coat and a suicide note at the base of the "H," she continued to climb—this time up the rungs of a maintenance worker's ladder that had been left propped against the back of the letter.

No one knows if Peg paused even once in her deadly mission. Perhaps she cast an eye out across the twinkling lights of the community below her. All that is known for certain is that she threw herself from the lethal perch onto the rocks below. The momentum of the plunge carried her down the slope until a clump of cactus bushes finally broke her fall. Her body, by then as badly broken as her spirit had been, was not spotted until early Monday morning. Incredibly, Peg Entwistle was not dead when she was found. Patient nurses spent hours pulling cactus spines out of Peg's body with tweezers, but Entwistle died of massive internal injuries before they could complete the task.

In an odd way, this same broken spirit has made Peg Entwistle a Hollywood legend. Her ghost haunts the hills around the sign, and also the Beachwood Canyon drugstore that she visited just before embarking on her terrible climb. The drugstore is gone now, replaced by a coffee shop, but the building is still haunted. Waitresses report that after closing, when all the customers have left, they'll occasionally feel a sudden chill as though someone had just entered the locked café.

The only person to ever report actually seeing Peg's ghost near the building was a waitress who had known the late actress years before. Before her own death in the early 1980s, Adeline Daniels often spoke of the evening that she heard a knock on the store's window, looked up, and clearly saw Peg Entwistle's ghostly image waving to her from the sidewalk.

More commonly, however, Peg is seen near the Hollywood sign, where she is always wearing the same white dress she wore on the night she killed herself. Several hikers, including long-time area resident Arthur Sellers, have watched in fascination as a vaporous image climbs the hill. All who have witnessed the sighting remark that they were sure the vision was not a living human being because her clothing and her stance as she made her way up the hillside were wrong for both the terrain and the weather.

Lew Pipes, who has lived in the area for more than 20 years, reported that he frequently took a neighbor's dog with him during an early morning exercise routine in the Hollywood Hills. On one occasion, the dog reacted very strangely. Although Lew saw nothing himself, he wondered if the dog had seen, or in some other way sensed, Peg Entwistle's restless spirit. The dog, who was used to hiking in the area with Lew, began "acting funny, like somebody was right there with us."

Moments later, the dog began purposefully trotting up the slope, hurrying away from the man who was walking him. The animal seemed to be following someone, while at the same time "keeping his distance." The normally obedient dog would not come when Pipes called him, so the man had no alternative but to follow. By the time he caught up to the animal, the man was badly out of breath and the dog was sitting at the base of the letter "H," staring intently down the hill. Seconds later, the dog looked up and resumed his role of exercise companion.

Some say that Peg Entwistle's ghost is doomed to walk the earth until the sign that she used as a suicide device is taken down. Surely there is an equally strong possibility that her spirit is now enjoying the fame that eluded her in life.

Spook High

Some types of institutions seem to be especially prone to hauntings. Hospitals, theaters and hotels are three that come quickly to mind. In addition, students often claim that the school they attend is haunted. And sometimes they're right.

"Home of the Sheiks" proclaims the sign overlooking the athletic field at Hollywood High School. The school mascots, the Sheiks, have been named as a tribute to the phenomenon that one movie and one actor playing a single great role can create—Rudolph Valentino's silhouette is emblazoned across an outer wall at the back of the building overlooking the sports field. The clear implication is that the movie and its star were winners. By extension, therefore, so will be the teams from Hollywood High.

Considering the rambling two-story school's location at the heart of the film community on Highland Avenue between Sunset Boulevard and Hollywood Boulevard, it is not surprising that Hollywood High's past and present

At haunted Hollywood High, not all the alumni have left school.

focus is on dramatic arts. As a result, the school has considerable historical and cultural significance, as well as a star-studded alumni list that includes names like Carol Burnett, Ricky and David Nelson, Stephanie Powers, John Ritter, Jason Robards and James Garner.

Students generally attend the school for three or four years. The teachers' tenure is usually somewhat longer. Legend has it, however, that at least three souls have made Hollywood High School their very permanent home and, in doing so, have turned these hallowed halls of learning into haunted halls.

A female student, upset at having failed a test, apparently killed herself in a fit of depression. Whether her soul regrets that decision or whether she just enjoys the atmosphere provided by this unique school, her spirit is said to remain at Hollywood High. She seems oblivious to today's world. Ironically, for someone who was so very dissatisfied with her life, she seems to have changed very little in her afterlife and simply goes about her day-to-day student activities as though she were still a student.

The story behind the school's young male ghost is much the same. It is said that he shot himself some years ago, but that his presence can still be felt around the school. The most protective entity of the three is the teacher who haunts the Green Room in the wing of the school set aside for dramatic productions. Although it's not known how the teacher met his demise, it is believed that he has stayed in the school to keep a watchful eye on students and, if possible, to prevent harm from coming to any of them.

As with most school hauntings, no one need fear the ghosts at spirit-filled school. They are not there to frighten or disrupt anyone. Hollywood High School is merely the place they have chosen to spend their eternities.

Act **5**

HOLLYWOOD

Ghostly Graveyards

Playbill

Marilyn Monroe (1926-1962)

Monkey Business (1952)

How to Marry a Millionaire (1953)

Niagara (1953)

Gentlemen Prefer Blondes (1953)

The Seven Year Itch (1955)

Bus Stop (1956)

The Prince and the Showgirl (1957)

The Asphalt Jungle (1957)

Some Like It Hot (1959)

The Misfits (1961)

Dominique Dunne (1959-1982)

Diary of a Teenage Hitchhiker (1979)

*The Haunting of
Harrington House* (1981)

Poltergeist (1982)

Heather O'Rourke (1975-1988)

Poltergeist (1982)

Poltergeist II: The Other Side (1986)

Poltergeist III (1988)

Richard Conte (1910-1975)

Guadalcanal Diary (1943)

13 Rue Madeleine (1946)

New York Confidential (1955)

I'll Cry Tomorrow (1955)

Ocean's Eleven (1960)

*Who's Been Sleeping in
My Bed?* (1963)

Circus World (1964)

The Greatest Story Ever Told (1964)

Assault on a Queen (1966)

Tony Rome (1967)

Lady in Cement (1968)

The Godfather (1972)

Rudolph Valentino (1895–1926)

*The Four Horsemen of
the Apocalypse* (1921)

The Sheik (1921)

Blood and Sand (1922)

Monsieur Beaucaire (1924)

The Eagle (1925)

Son of the Sheik (1926)

Clifton Webb (1889–1966)

Laura (1944)

The Razor's Edge (1946)

Mr. Belvedere Goes to College (1949)

Cheaper by the Dozen (1950)

Stars and Stripes Forever (1952)

Titanic (1953)

Three Coins in the Fountain (1954)

**Roscoe "Fatty" Arbuckle
(1887-1933)**

Tillie's Punctured Romance (1914)

Miss Fatty's Seaside Loves (1915)

Fatty's Tintype Tangle (1915)

Fatty and Mabel Adrift (1916)

A Creampuff Romance (1916)

A Reckless Romeo (1917)

Out West (1918)

The Roundup (1920)

Brewster's Millions (1920)

Traveling Salesman (1921)

Gasoline Gus (1921)

Crazy to Marry (1921)

Graveyards of the Rich and Famous

Cemetery tours in Hollywood have become almost as popular with tourists as studio tours. Every week, fans from all over the world visit the former stars' supposedly final resting places. Some of those deceased, however, are not doing much resting. As a result, the graveyards in Tinseltown are very haunted places.

* * *

The entrance to Westwood Memorial Park on Glendon Avenue in Los Angeles is easy to miss. It's just a driveway tucked between two commercial buildings. That somewhat obscure and definitely ordinary-looking entryway leads to perhaps the most popular gravesite in all of North America—that of Marilyn Monroe.

The tragic beauty's remains are entombed in a chamber that resembles dozens of others in the beautifully maintained grounds. Like the others, Marilyn Monroe's resting place is marked only by a simple brass identification marker. There are, however, some differences that make Monroe's grave stand out from the others. In addition to an ever-present bouquet, the vault's stone surface is discolored and worn from thousands of hands caressing it and even kissing it. Imprints from lips dot the cold, flat façade. These signs are evidence of the

The apparition of screen legend Marilyn Monroe occasionally visits the spot where her body was laid to rest.

actress's enduring—if not increasing—popularity, and are an amazing tribute to a woman who died in 1962.

Most days, that's pretty much all there is to be seen at that particular vault. Occasionally, though, a vaporous image will hover nearby. Some witnesses believe this is the ghost of Marilyn Monroe. During her short, sad life, Marilyn always loved to have her picture taken. Apparently, death hasn't changed that. Of the hundreds of thousands of photographs that have been taken at her grave, a few have actually captured the voluptuous blonde's filmy apparition as she visits with and poses for those who have come to pay their respects.

* * *

In the same section of Westwood Memorial Park are two even more poignant tombs—those of Dominique Dunne, who played the role of eldest child Dana Freeling in the original *Poltergeist* movie, and Heather O'Rourke, the little blonde girl who played the role of youngest daughter Carol Anne in all three installments of the horror flick trilogy. Bouquets of fresh flowers decorate both graves. Heather's resting place is also marked with photographs and toys.

Persistent rumors connect these two premature deaths to what has become known as the "*Poltergeist* curse." People who worked on the films complained of uncomfortable,

Beautiful young actress Dominique Dunne was strangled by a jealous boyfriend. Was she a victim of the Poltergeist *curse?*

Heather O'Rourke's grave is decorated with toys. Some say the child star died as a result of a curse on the cast and crew of the film Poltergeist, *in which she and Dominique Dunne appeared as members of a family plagued by ghosts.*

eerie feelings during production. The year the first film was released, 23-year-old Dominique Dunne was strangled to death by her jealous boyfriend. Then, the year after *Poltergeist III* was completed, Heather O'Rourke died of a strange and sudden intestinal blockage. Since that time, urban legends have insisted that the film series was haunted by the ghosts it sought to depict.

* * *

Close to Dominique Dunne's resting place lies a slightly whimsical grave marker. The grave of actor Richard Conte is marked in traditional fashion with the traditional years of birth and death. That last date, however, is followed by a

What is implied by the question mark after the date of death on Richard Conte's headstone? Did the actor stop walking the earth in 1975 or not at all? Many believe that his ghost is the shadowy form seen hovering around a nearby tree.

question mark, as if openly debating the reality of his death. The person who arranged for the strange inscription on the marker may have been quite correct to do so. Visitors to the cemetery have reported seeing a vaporous apparition near a tree that grows by the grave. It's possible that the ghost is Conte's and that he's still enjoying himself in this world.

* * *

Anonymous, unmarked plots in Forest Lawn cemetery are now homes to the bodies of Errol Flynn, Clark Gable, Carole Lombard, Mary Pickford, Lucille Ball and Jean Harlow. Their spirits, however, do not haunt the graveyard but apparently prefer to haunt their former Hollywood-area homes instead.

This is the tree around which witnesses report seeing the hovering ghost of a man who may be actor Richard Conte.

* * *

Not all of Hollywood's ghosts are human, as the local pet cemetery attests. The ghost of Rudolph Valentino's favorite dog, a Great Dane named Kabar, is alleged to romp among the gravestones here.

* * *

Hollywood Forever is the oldest cemetery in the community, even pre-dating the movie industry by 20 years. Kabar's owner, Rudolph Valentino, is one of the many stars buried here. His ghost is occasionally seen in the graveyard, probably as it makes its way to the adjacent Paramount costume department, where the apparition is reportedly seen every now and again.

Douglas Fairbanks and "Bugsy" Siegel are two other spirits who refuse to rest in peace, but it's usually their homes and not their gravesites in Hollywood Forever that they haunt. Clifton Webb's ghost, however, has been known to haunt both his former home and the area around his burial plot in this well-established depository for corporeal remains.

* * *

The films of Roscoe "Fatty" Arbuckle have been nearly forgotten now, but the 300-pound comedian was one of the brightest stars of the silent era. At the height of his fame, Arbuckle pulled down $10,000 for a day's work—and while that may still sound like a nice chunk of change, it was a truly astronomical figure in those days. He was second in popularity only to his friend Charlie Chaplin (the two appeared together in quite a few movies, including the 1914 classic *Tillie's Punctured Romance*) and he was generous about discovering and nurturing other great film talents, such as Buster Keaton. The work of Arbuckle's friends and colleagues not only survives but finds new admirers with each passing year; sadly, Fatty himself was relegated to the dustbins of Hollywood history when his career, his reputation and his life were permanently destroyed by scandal on September 5, 1921. If Fatty is remembered at all today, it is usually because his name comes up as part of a gruesome urban legend, one that has doggedly refused to die long after all of those involved in that long-ago scandal have passed on.

After signing a new million-dollar contract with Paramount Pictures, Fatty celebrated by taking a holiday to San Francisco over the Labor Day weekend of 1921. Arbuckle's long-time associate Fred Fishback decided to help his friend relax by throwing a lavish party, complete with bathtub gin (this was, after all, the era of Prohibition), in adjoining suites 1219, 1220 and 1221 at the luxurious St. Francis Hotel. A bit-part actress-cum-prostitute named Virginia Rappé crashed the party along with her associate Maude Delmont, a truly unsavory character against whom California police had filed more than four dozen counts of extortion, bigamy, fraud and racketeering. Neither Rappé nor Delmont were invited to the party by Arbuckle. In fact, Arbuckle voiced concern about Rappé and Delmont being present, worried that their notoriety with the police might cause the party to be raided.

At 3:00 PM, Arbuckle decided he'd had enough of the party. When he tried to enter his adjoining suite, he found Virginia Rappé passed out on the bathroom floor in a puddle of her own vomit. Arbuckle picked Rappé up and placed her on the bed. She regained conciousness and asked for a glass of water, which he gave her. At 3:10 PM, Arbuckle left—fully clothed—and ran to Room 1220 to get help. When he returned with others, they found Virginia Rappé fully clothed and shrieking in pain.

Arbuckle and the others applied ice to Rappé's abdomen in an effort to reduce her fever. Realizing that something was seriously wrong with Rappé, members of the party called the hotel management, and the woman was taken to a nearby hospital. Four days later, she died of peritonitis, brought on by a rupture of her fallopian tubes, complicated by an advanced case of venereal disease.

But Maude Delmont, who had guzzled more than ten shots of liquor before passing out at the party, had a different explanation for Virginia's death: She went to the San Francisco Police and filed charges claiming that Roscoe Arbuckle had caused Rappé's death with a brutal sexual assault.

Although an autopsy revealed absolutely no physical evidence of a sexual attack, and although police inquiry established that the woman had an extremely shady background—a known history of prostitution, the little matter of her having endured five back-alley abortions before the age of sixteen, and the fact that she currently suffered from syphilis, a disease that in all likelihood had caused the lethal rupture—the press immediately sensationalized the story, suggesting that the corpulent Arbuckle had caused the rupture by raping a poor, innocent starlet, and in some particularly lurid accounts, by violating Rappé with a champagne bottle.

William Randolph Hearst's yellow journalism painted Arbuckle as a slobbering, manslaughtering rapist and the poster boy for Hollywood's threat to the moral fabric of America. Years later, Hearst bragged to a mortified Buster Keaton that he had sold more papers with the Arbuckle story than he had after the sinking of the *Lusitania*. The public reaction to these headline stories was as immediate as it was harsh. Women's groups across the United States loudly condemned Arbuckle for his "immorality." As far as the public was concerned, Roscoe Arbuckle had already been found guilty of murder. His films were yanked from theaters across the country, never to return.

Arbuckle endured three trials before being acquitted in 1922. His wife, Minta Durfee, stood by him throughout the seemingly endless legal process. The first two trials ended in hung juries—a Mrs. Helen Hubbard, who was the hold-out during the second trial, bragged that no one could change her mind and that she had intended to vote for conviction from the moment she'd heard Arbuckle had been arrested! However, the third jury deliberated for less than a minute and included the following official apology with the verdict:

"Acquittal is not enough for Roscoe Arbuckle. We feel that a great injustice has been done him. We feel also that it was only our plain duty to give him this exoneration, under the evidence, for there was not the slightest proof to connect him in an way with the commission of a crime. He was manly throughout the case, and told a straightforward story on the witness stand, which we all believed. The happening at the hotel was an unfortunate affair for which Arbuckle, so the evidence shows, was in no way responsible. We wish him success and hope that the American people will take the judgment of 14 men and women who have sat listening for 31 days to the evidence, that Roscoe Arbuckle is entirely innocent and free of all blame."

But Arbuckle's acquittal hardly mattered in the end. He became a scapegoat for the Bible-thumping moralists behind the newly formed Hays Office (a censorship bureau that sought to monitor Hollywood's morally suspect stars). Despite being banned from the screen, Arbuckle managed to get work writing gags and directing the occasional short film for friends like Buster Keaton. In these cases, he usually hid under the pointed pseudonym William B. Good. Unfortunately, Arbuckle took to easing his sorrows with large doses of alcohol after his career was destroyed, and he died at the age of 46 in 1933.

While there have never been any reports of Fatty's ghost, Rappé's afterlife has been a long and active one. Nighttime visitors to the historic Hollywood Forever cemetery have heard plaintive sobbing coming from the area around the woman's plot. Most people who hear the disembodied weeping come away convinced that Virginia Rappé's ghostly cries are an attempt to tell her side of the sordid story.

* * *

If a mysterious death is one of the reasons that a spirit lingers on earth, then the male ghost in Hollywood's oldest graveyard might be that of William Desmond Taylor.

The morning of Thursday, February 2, 1922, dawned sunny and bright in Los Angeles. But the city's lovely weather was somewhat wasted on the dozen or so folks scurrying around the Alavarado Court apartment complex. And weather, lovely or otherwise, would never again have an impact on one Hollywood citizen—esteemed director William Desmond Taylor lay dead on the floor of unit 404.

Taylor's murder caused a flurry of activity both before and after the police arrived to begin their investigation. It seemed that there was much that Paramount Pictures executives wanted to conceal about their company's former golden boy. Toward that end, half a dozen people were busily going through desk drawers and destroying many of the papers they found stored in them.

Today, with the advantage of hindsight, it might appear that the group of worried people were overreacting. Of course, they had no idea how badly Taylor's bisexuality might reflect upon Paramount if it became common knowledge. As far as they knew, Taylor had nothing else that needed to be hidden, so their efforts were directly solely toward sanitizing the apartment of all signs of sexual activity.

Taylor had arrived in Hollywood in 1912 at the age of 40. While establishing himself in his new milieu, he apparently forgot to mention a few things about his background, such as the fact that his real name was William Cunningham Deane-Tanner and that he was the married father of a four-year-old daughter. Taylor's selective memory didn't seem to effect his ability to get on with his new life in the movies. He quickly won acting roles in silent films before being given the privilege of directing. Taylor was a good director—a natural. It was immediately clear that he'd found his calling, and he went on to direct highly success-ful silent versions of *Tom Sawyer*, *Huckleberry Finn* and *Davy Crockett.*

By coincidence, he'd also found a new woman to love. The devoted couple, like tens of thousands of others around the world, had to put their romance on hold while the First World War raged around them. Taylor joined the Canadian Army and was sent away—but, by luck of timing, was never called upon to fight. In 1918, he was back in Hollywood, having forgotten about his former love, but more than ready to direct the first film based on Lucy Maud Montgomery's *Anne of Green Gables.*

The choice for the actress to play the role of Anne was made extremely carefully. When 17-year-old Mary Miles Minter won the audition, everyone was initially delighted. At the time, studio executives had no way of knowing that the girl was accompanied by a Stage Mother from Hell. Mrs. Minter was controlling, manipulative and very much an influence on her daughter. As if this situation wasn't diffi-cult enough, young Mary decided that she'd fallen in love with the movie's director, William D. Taylor. He was 30 years her senior and did not reciprocate her affections.

As a matter of fact, Taylor was, by this time, dating yet another woman, popular movie comedian Mabel Normand, who was perhaps as well known for her raging cocaine addiction as for her work on the screen. Trouble was clearly about to brew in that particular lovers' paradise because Taylor was vehemently opposed to the drug abuse he saw spreading through the movie industry. He was legitimately fond of Normand and blamed her drug supplier for her addiction. Taylor took it upon himself to confront the pusher, and the two men had a vicious argument.

Taylor may have disapproved of drug use but he apparently had no moral qualms with sending his gay valet out to pick up young men and bring them home to satisfy that aspect of his sexual preferences. The valet, a man named Henry Peavey, had replaced a former employee, also a homosexual. That employee, whose name was Edward F. Sands, had abruptly left Taylor's employment about a year before, taking with him the director's new sports car and $4,000 in cash.

As part of their investigation into Taylor's death, the police questioned his neighbors. Mrs. Faith MacLean admitted hearing what she thought was a car backfiring. She immediately went to the window and looked out. She couldn't see a car, just a person coming out of Taylor's suite. According to the information she gave investigators, the person was "dressed like a man, but funny looking, and walked like a woman."

The police proceeded with this case as they would with any murder case, by drawing up a list of suspects. Less than a year later, the list of people who had both motive and opportunity to kill William Taylor contained 200 names. Despite this impressively long list, no one was ever charged with the murder.

William Taylor's effect on those closest to him—which included all of the suspects in his murder—didn't seem to end with the director's mortal heartbeat. In fact, his death seemed to leave behind a deadly curse.

Edward F. Sands, the employee who stole Taylor's car and money, killed himself only weeks after Taylor's murder.

Mabel Normand died as a result of her drug addiction. She was only 37 years old.

Henry Peavey lived his last days in a flophouse, where he died a badly broken man in 1937.

Mary Miles Minter never worked again. She was a hermit and completely insane by the time she died in 1984.

Mary's mother fought off a series of lawsuits from her daughter over a period of many years and eventually died a pauper.

Given the long and likely list of suspects, why was no one ever charged with the murder? Byron Fitts, the last surviving official involved with the case, could perhaps have answered that question. Unfortunately, he killed himself in 1973 without ever having shed light on the mystery.

It seems to me that William Desmond Taylor's spirit has every reason to restlessly roam the area near where his body is buried.

Act 6

HOLLYWOOD

Stage Fright

Playbill

Victor Kilian (1891-1979)

The Adventures of Tom Sawyer (1938)

The Adventures of Huckleberry Finn (1939)

Only Angels Have Wings (1939)

Doctor Cyclops (1940)

Sergeant York (1941)

This Gun for Hire (1942)

The Ox-Bow Incident (1943)

Dangerous Passage (1944)

I Shot Jesse James (1949)

Unknown World (1950)

Mary Hartman, Mary Hartman (TV series, 1976)

Howard Hughes (as producer and/or director) (1905-1976)

Hell's Angels (1930)

Scarface (1932)

The Outlaw (1943)

The Conqueror (1956)

Jet Pilot (1957)

William Holden (1918-1981)

Our Town (1940)

Sunset Blvd. (1950)

Born Yesterday (1950)

Stalag 17 (1953)

The Bridges at Toko-Ri (1954)

Sabrina (1954)

Picnic (1956)

The Bridge on the River Kwai (1957)

The World of Suzie Wong (1960)

Casino Royale (1967)

The Wild Bunch (1969)

The Blue Knight (TV mini-series, 1973)

The Towering Inferno (1974)

Network (1976)

S.O.B. (1981)

Rudolph Valentino (1895–1926)

The Four Horsemen of the Apocalypse (1921)

The Sheik (1921)

Blood and Sand (1922)

Monsieur Beaucaire (1924)

The Eagle (1925)

Son of the Sheik (1926)

Lon Chaney, Sr. (1883-1930)

Treasure Island (1920)

Oliver Twist (1922)

Shadows (1922)

The Hunchback of Notre Dame (1923)

The Phantom of the Opera (1925)

The Monster (1925)

Mr. Wu (1927)

London After Midnight (1927)

West of Zanzibar (1928)

Laugh, Clown, Laugh (1928)

While the City Sleeps (1928)

The Unholy Three (1930)

The Eccentric Ghost of Howard Hughes

Power corrupts. Absolute power corrupts absolutely. And in Hollywood, as elsewhere, money is power. In 1924, when 19-year-old Howard Hughes arrived in the capital of the movie-making industry, he took the town by storm. This wasn't much of a surprise, because he really did "have it all." He was young, handsome, extremely rich and very interested in getting involved with the film industry. That interest included seducing as many of the beautiful women in Tinseltown as possible. Toward *that* end, if Hughes was interested in a woman who was currently dating a star, he would simply arrange for that star to be offered a lucrative role in a movie being filmed in a faraway location, thus leaving the star's former girlfriend free to be courted. Or so the rumors went. Possibly using that method and possibly using others, Howard Hughes was known to have been involved with Jane Russell, Katharine Hepburn, Olivia de Havilland, Mitzi Gaynor, Gina Lollobrigida, Ginger Rogers, Hedy Lamarr, Ava Gardner, Carole Lombard and Jean Harlow, among others.

By the time Hughes was in his mid-20s, he had begun to turn his professional attention away from the movies and on to another endeavor that fascinated him—the burgeoning aircraft business. Here, too, he was initially successful, setting a world speed record of 325 miles per hour in 1935, while flying a plane he had designed himself. By the early 1940s he was back to directing movies while continuing to maintain his involvement in aeronautics. But not all of those projects were to prove as successful as his initial foray into the field. For example, his enormous all-wood airplane, *The Spruce Goose*, virtually defined the term "white elephant." He crashed the plane in 1946 and suffered many serious injuries, including severe trauma to his head. The corruption of Hughes's sanity had apparently begun. From that point on, Howard Hughes's personality quirks became not only more bizarre but also much more difficult to hide.

Hughes became increasingly preoccupied with cleanliness and pathologically concerned about his health. His dislike for insects progressed to a phobia of products created from or by living creatures. As a result, he preferred to be nude rather than wear wool (made from sheep, which he felt were repulsively dirty animals) or silk (which, of course, was made by worms) or even cotton (which he reasoned could carry germs).

In 1949, despite his slipping hold on sanity, Howard Hughes continued to transact business. Through one of those transactions, he took ownership of the Pantages Theater on Hollywood Boulevard. Despite the difficulties presented by his growing paranoia and hypochondria, Hughes established and worked out of an office on the second floor of the theater building. By 1958, however, his mental deterioration was extremely serious. He was prescribed various medications; unfortunately, the huge quantities of pills only increased his problems by making him a drug addict. Hughes soon became a complete recluse, never again appearing in public.

Despite all his supposed ailments and his very strange, unhealthy habits such as abusing drugs, Hughes lived until

The Pantages Theatre is haunted by the ghost of its former owner, eccentric multi-millionaire Howard Hughes, as well as by the spirit of a female singer.

1976. Fittingly, he died in an airplane. His spirit, however, is thought by some to have remained at the Pantages Theater. Hughes was a heavy smoker and people have reported detecting the smell of cigarette smoke in the empty room that was once his office. Inexplicable drafts suddenly waft through the room when there's no known reason for such currents.

Howard Hughes's desk in his theater office had distinctive brass handles on the drawers. The phantom sounds of those knobs clinking against the wood of the drawer fronts have been reported. When Hughes's ghost is seen, it's apparent that he's not aware of renovations to the building, because the route taken by his apparition leads through a door that no longer exists. In other words, he walks through a solid wall and out of sight!

After a break-in and some ensuing vandalism occurred at the theater in 1990, employees reported a change in the atmosphere, especially in the balcony area where most of the damage took place. For months after, angry phantom sounds could be heard throughout the area.

Although Hughes's spirit might not know it, he is not alone in his theatrical hereafter. A ghostly legend dating back to the early 1930s indicates that a woman's voice can be heard singing in the Pantages. The musical manifestation is thought to be that of a patron who aspired to a career on the stage. Her spirit's voice is clearly not a figment of anyone's imagination because it was once picked up and carried throughout the theater when the microphone system was turned on.

The identity of the ghost who helped a current-day employee of the theater's costume department is not known. It might have been the lady singer, it might have been Howard Hughes, or there might even be a *third* phantom lurking about. Whichever the case, as the woman was trying to get out of the theater in the dark and stumbling ineffectively through the building, a guiding hand took her by the elbow and led her to a door.

The woman opened the door, thus letting in more than enough light for her to finally be able to see her surroundings. Unfortunately for her peace of mind, this meant she could see that she was entirely alone. There was no one near her who could have been keeping a hand on her elbow. It's anyone's guess who could have been helping the stranded wardrobe lady. If it was, in fact, the ghost of Howard Hughes, then it would seem he's considerably less reclusive, and hopefully happier, in death than he was in life.

Phantom of the Playhouse

I had been given to understand that the Pasadena Playhouse—California's official State Theater, located in North Hollywood—was haunted. My information was somewhat old, though, so I thought it would be wise to check with the theater's administration to make sure my story was still accurate. Theater archivist Ellen Bailey kindly replied to my query with the simple statement, "Yes, Gilmor's ghost is still here."

The "Gilmor" to which Ellen Bailey refers is Gilmor Brown, the man who founded the Pasadena Playhouse. Brown may have been in charge of theatrical operations when he was alive, but in death he seems to have accepted the fact that others must now run the show. If this weren't so, today's employees at the Playhouse would have a much tougher time doing their various jobs. None of the employees has ever said that they mind having a ghost on the site, but I'm sure they're all grateful that he makes himself scarce when they need him to.

You see, Gilmor Brown seems to be something of a practical joker. When members of the staff find a personal belonging out of place, they know not to worry. Nothing's been stolen—it's only the resident phantom playing games with his flesh-and-blood counterparts. The missing object inevitably turns up in an inappropriate location not long after.

During his life, Gilmor Brown's office was located on the building's third floor. Today, when current staff members are riding the elevator, it will often stop at the third floor and the doors will open. No one, either inside or outside the elevator, has pushed a button to make the car stop, but it stops all the same. By now, people just assume that they are experiencing another case of Gilmor's ghost wanting to get to or from his old office.

In common with many phantoms, Brown's spirit is attracted to things electric or electronic. For example, the theater's house lights will mysteriously turn on at a specific moment every week. When lighting experts were called in to investigate, they found no mechanical or electrical reason for this anomalous occurrence.

The only time that the resident wraith really caused a problem was when technicians, in anticipation of a forthcoming show, had carefully set the controls in the overhead booth before leaving—and locking—the area so they could then take a break. When they returned, all of their painstaking and detailed work had been rearranged. Puzzled, they reset their controls. This time, in addition to locking the control room door, they posted an usher outside the booth

to act as a guard. Some time later, when the sound technicians returned, the usher assured them that no one had
been near their workspace—and yet, once again the controls had been rearranged.

Fortunately, all that's necessary to control Gilmor's
ghostly hijinks is for a worker who has been the brunt of a
trick to issue an ever-so-gentle rebuke to the spirit. Simply
saying out loud, "That's enough, Gilmor" or "Not now, I'm
too busy" seems to be sufficient to put an end to the antics
and to allow the employee to get on with his or her work.

Knowing that the ghost is obedient would certainly
reduce a great deal of the strain involved in working in a
haunted theater such as the beautiful old Pasadena
Playhouse. And what a happy coincidence that is, because
it's more than obvious that Gilmor Brown still enjoys the
association with the theater to which he devoted so much of
his life.

Studio Specters

Without Hollywood's film production studios, the movie industry as we know it today would never have evolved. They are so important to those involved in show business that countless lives, careers and fortunes have been made and broken in the various studio buildings. Given the intensity of emotions experienced and exhibited in these places over the years, it is not surprising that many of the studios are haunted.

William Holden's long, distinguished career on the silver screen stretched from his inauspicious debut as "Inmate" in the 1938 potboiler *Prison Farm* to a memorable starring turn in his final film, writer-director Blake Edwards's savage 1981 Hollywood satire *S.O.B.* In the 43 years between those two milestones he acted in more than 70 films, including such classics as *Our Town, Born Yesterday, Picnic, The Bridge on the River Kwai* and *The Wild Bunch.* He won an Academy Award for his role in 1953's *Stalag 17* and was nominated two other times, for 1950's *Sunset Blvd.* and 1976's *Network.* He also won an Emmy for his powerful performance as an aging cop in the 1973 mini-series *The Blue Knight.* Holden was not only an enduring (and accomplished) actor, but he fought tirelessly against the studio system to secure better conditions for his colleagues as the first vice-president of the Screen Actors Guild. Later in life, he devoted much of his time to raising public awareness about the need to protect endangered wildlife.

Sadly, Holden died on November 16, 1981 at the age of 62 at his home in Santa Monica due to an accidental fall

William Holden

The revenant of Academy Award-winning actor William Holden has been thought to linger in part of this CBS Studio ever since a séance was held to contact Holden in the afterlife.

while drunk; the actor had battled alcoholism for many years. His ashes were scattered in the Pacific Ocean, but, because his demise was so sudden, the actor must have felt that he had unfinished business here on earth. Duncan St. James, owner and operator of ghost-friendly TourLand USA, explains that not long after the memorial services for Holden were held, the deceased paid a visit to a CBS television studio. "Holden's lifelong friend Hal Cope was present at the studios, where they held a séance," St. James said. "Holden must have wanted to come back to let everyone know that he was fine. Information that was not publicly known was received by the parapsychologists present at the séance, and Hal Cope was there to verify that the spirit was indeed that of his late friend."

* * *

The story behind at least one of the ghosts at Culver City's Culver Studios is a tragic one. Thomas Ince started the business in 1918. Six years later he was dead—murdered, according to one spin, while attending a party aboard powerful newspaper magnate William Randolph Hearst's yacht. Hearst, this version maintains, thought Ince was kissing Marion Davies, Hearst's longtime paramour. If that spin on the events is true, Ince became the victim of a fatal case of mistaken identity. The rest of the gossip that survives from that night indicates that it was not Thomas Ince but Charlie Chaplin who was romancing Davies at the time.

That rumor, however, is somewhat suspect because it also goes on to explain that syndicated newspaper columnist Louella Parsons got her start in the gossip column business as an incentive from Hearst for keeping quiet about the shipboard killing she'd witnessed. A contradictory version of the events has Louella Parsons on the other side of the country in New York, attending a movie premiere at the time Ince was murdered. Another version of the truth also begins with the parties on Hearst's yacht, but this twist indicates that, although Hearst was displeased with the fact that Thomas Ince would be directing Marion Davies in a movie role, Ince simply dropped dead after consuming a toast celebrating this assignment.

Whichever of the seemingly endless variations of the story one subscribes to, the movie studio business Thomas Ince began did not die with him. Under new owners, the Culver Studios continued to flourish after its founder's death. Many classic films, such as *Gone with the Wind*, have been shot there. Perhaps part of the credit for that success should remain with the deceased and his influence from beyond—because a ghostly image of a man wearing a bowler hat and matching Ince's description has been seen entering the room that used to be the entrepreneur's private projection suite.

During the summer of 1988, while major renovations were going on at the studio, this apparition was seen several times. Workers spotted the ghost on a catwalk above a stage. It was so real-looking that the witnesses called out to the image. Seconds later, those employees knew they had not encountered a trespasser, but rather the ghost of the company's founder. Even if they had not recognized the revenant's description from the long-standing ghost stories told around the place, they realized that this was not a living human being when it glided to the end of the catwalk and disappeared through a wall.

Some weeks later, in another stage area, the ghost again appeared briefly. This time, before he walked through another wall, he spoke, apparently expressing his opinion on the changes being made to the building. His message was short and to the point: "I don't like what you're doing to my studio," he said simply.

Thomas Ince is not alone beyond the veil at Culver Studios. As of yet no one's been able to determine who the female ghost haunting the place might be, even though she has also allowed herself to be seen. Those who have not been quick enough to catch a glimpse of her still know when she's been around because she leaves behind a ghostly trademark—pockets of inexplicably cold air.

* * *

Paramount Studios, located on Gower Street in Hollywood, is the part-time home to one of the most enduring and ubiquitous ghosts in show business—the spirit of Rudolph Valentino. Fittingly, his luminescent apparition haunts the section of the costume department where the period apparel is stored.

There is also at least one haunted catwalk at Paramount. Footsteps are frequently heard echoing across the ledge above the stage at Paramount's Studio 5 when the area is known to be vacant. While those sounds are heard, a form can occasionally also be seen, but not clearly enough for anyone to make out who the spirit might have been in life.

Another ghost who is sometimes encountered at Paramount is not thought to have been associated with the studio. It's assumed that this ghost's earthly remains are buried in a nearby cemetery. Occasionally, it would seem that this entity makes a wrong turn and ends up in the studio. When this happens, the poor soul looks extremely confused before disappearing through a wall and out of sight again.

* * *

Located on the south side of Melrose Avenue directly across the street from Paramount, little-known Raleigh Studios is one of the oldest Hollywood movie studios. The business began in February of 1915 but probably wasn't haunted until 1932, when an electrician suffered a fatal accident on the job. He had been making his way along a catwalk when he lost his footing and fell to his death on the stage floor below. Psychics who have toured the area where he died have all experienced the distinct impression of someone falling over backwards.

The electrician's ghost is generally a protective presence but, in true ghostly fashion, has also been credited with causing power failures and sudden localized drops in temperature. Security guards have reported hearing phantom music coming from areas of the building known to be empty, and heavy pieces of equipment that are left in a specific location will turn up somewhere else, despite the fact that no one has been near them.

In the early 1970s, after two workers had locked up the sound stages, they heard a voice call to them. Because the men had assumed that they were alone, the words startled them and they stopped dead in their tracks. When they'd regained a bit of their composure, they called out. No one answered, but a 300-pound lighting fixture began to sway in an arc that they later estimated to be between six and eight feet in circumference. Not feeling the least bit comfortable with the thoughts of what they might be witnessing, the men quickly secured the area and left.

* * *

Productions of *The Phantom of the Opera* have been entertaining audiences for years. As far back as 1925, horror actor Lon Chaney played the title role for a Universal Studios production. Stage 28, on which that early rendition of the enduring story was filmed, has long been haunted by a ghost wearing a dark cape. The image first appeared shortly after Lon Chaney's death in 1930. His presence is so strong that, in addition to studio employees, even visitors have been known to spot the phantom as he runs along a catwalk high above the stage. At the same time, doors will often mysteriously open and close and lights will just as mysteriously turn on and off.

In addition, many workers have reported encountering what they believe is a former electrician's spirit. It is said that he died as a result of a fall from a catwalk and that his spirit has never left that elevated platform.

Anyone familiar with either show business or ghost-lore will completely understand why these studios tend to be so haunted. The energy of the souls who have gone before simply continues to resonate throughout the studio buildings.

Magically Appearing

The Magic Castle would be an interesting place even if it weren't haunted. Perched atop a hill at the corner of Franklin Avenue and Orange Drive, the beautiful Victorian mansion is located a stone's throw from the hustle and bustle of Hollywood Boulevard. Despite its status as a landmark site and its close proximity to other area attractions, most of the interior of The Magic Castle is off limits to the average tourist. The undeniably intriguing old building (it was erected in 1908) has been a private club since

This highly secretive private club is purportedly haunted by the protective ghost of a former employee.

Even in broad daylight, the mysterious Magic Castle gives the impression of being a haunted mansion.

1963—a club for magicians that is only open to magician-members and their invited guests. How fitting, then, that the venue is said to be haunted.

The ghost, according to a television documentary, is that of a former employee at the Castle—a bartender. His presence, which is always reported to be "reassuring," has actually been seen by current employees.

Ghosts Inside and Out

The façade of Mann's Chinese Theatre, and the sidewalk in front of it, are among the world's most recognizable landmarks. The ghost who haunts that famous area, however, is a relative newcomer to the Hollywood Boulevard theater. The ghost inside the theater has probably been there longer.

Originally Grauman's Chinese Theatre, the extravagant movie palace was built by master showman Sid Grauman in 1927 to host the premiere of Cecil B. DeMille's extravagant epic, *The King of Kings*. Grauman's unique choice of style for the building—a Chinese pagoda designed by famed architects Meyer and Holler—was intended to be similarly attention-grabbing. The Chinese Theatre has always been, and will no doubt always remain, utterly unique.

If architectural styling didn't guarantee this uniqueness, then silent-screen star Norma Talmadge's misstep, as she left the theater shortly after its opening, certainly did. Legend has it that Talmadge, unaware that cement had just been poured right outside the theater's lobby, stepped out through the front door and onto the sidewalk. Her shoes, of course, left a permanent impression in the still-wet concrete. That simple miscue apparently began a tradition that has resulted in one of Hollywood's most popular tourist attractions. Today, celebrities consider it a great honor to be invited to include both their hand- and footprints alongside

Just outside the entrance to Mann's Chinese Theatre, the ghost of actor Victor Kilian paces the sidewalk, looking for the man who murdered him. The sidewalk Kilian's specter travels is covered with the cement autographs, handprints and footprints of legendary Hollywood stars.

Hollywood legends and pioneers. As a result, dozens of squares of cement in front of Mann's Chinese Theatre are decorated with the names, shoeprints and handprints of more than seven decades of the most acclaimed movie stars.

The fans who flock to see their favorite film stars' impressions—and to see if their own hands and feet have comparable, star-like shapes and sizes—likely have no idea that the very area they're exclaiming over is haunted.

History tells us that, in 1982, while enjoying a drink at a local bar, television and movie actor Victor Kilian struck up a conversation with a stranger. Kilian evidently extended an invitation to continue the conversation at the actor's apartment. That friendly overture proved fatal—Kilian's badly beaten body was found the next day in his burglarized Yucca Street apartment, roughly a block from Mann's Chinese Theatre. Although his murderer has never been found, the deceased has apparently never given up his search for the man or men who killed him. It is said that Kilian's restless spirit paces a route encompassing the famous sidewalk squares in front of the famous landmark.

Rumor also has it that the interior of Mann's is haunted, too. It is believed that this little ghost may be Annabell, who spends most of her time across the street at the Vogue Theatre. Whatever her identity, the little wraith restricts her presence to the backstage area where she's said to occasionally tug at the stage curtain and to haunt the dressing room area.

Annabell and Friends

When it opened in 1936, the Vogue Theatre was a glamorous place. Being situated on Hollywood Boulevard meant it had the three most important real estate prerequisites—location, location, location— in spades. From its glittering, Depression-era opening night until the considerably less glittering night in the spring of 1992 when it closed its doors, the Vogue Theatre was an important show-business venue.

The theater sat dark almost exactly five years until it was taken over by a group known as the ISPR (International Society for Psychic Research) Investigative Team in 1997. The personable Daena Smoller and her partner, parapsychologist Dr. Larry Montz, intended to restore the building. In addition to supplying much-needed office space, they reasoned that the venue would be perfect for holding seminars and for hosting guest lecturers. Unfortunately, their plan never came to fruition.

"Once we found out how full of active spirits it was … we knew it wasn't really conducive, considering what we do," Daena Smoller recalled.

Not wanting to waste the interesting old property, Montz and Smoller invited a third partner, award-winning filmmaker Beeaje Quick, to join them. The old theater once again began to be used for its original purpose, among other things.

The ghosts at the Vogue Theatre are cherished by the venerable institution's current owners and operators.

"We used it for screenings for different movie studios. Last fall, the Vogue was one of the three primary venues for the American Film Institute's International Filmfest, so it got a lot of attention for that," Daena explained.

Immediately after describing this use of the theater, Daena added, "Annabell and her friends seemed to be happy." While that was nice for them, the information really did provoke more questions than provide answers. For instance, who are Annabell and her friends?

Daena further explained, "The children that are there died in 1901. Annabell told us about that. This was her schoolhouse. She gave us all kinds of wild information— the name of her school teacher, Miss Elizabeth. We did a few more investigations, got more solid information and were able to find the schoolhouse on this site, Prospect Elementary School, in the records—and it did burn down in 1901. Most of the children did die. Annabell died in the fire and now six of them seem to stay around."

Not surprisingly, because she is only a youngster, the ghost of Annabell is somewhat shy around adults and has confined her communication strictly to Daena, whom the child's spirit claims reminds her of "Miss Elizabeth." The little wraith explained to Daena that the theater was built, in part, on the ground where her schoolhouse had been located.

Annabell is not alone in her theatrical hereafter. Two little boys, both named Michael, and a girl named Jennifer also haunt the place. Fraternal twins Pamela and Peter have moved on by now.

In addition to the children's spirits, another two ghosts at the Vogue are adult males. One of those, Fritz, was a projectionist at the Vogue for many years. It is said that one afternoon while Fritz was working, he died of natural causes. Fritz's ghost only becomes agitated now if unprofessional people meddle in the areas that used to fall within his jurisdiction.

The other adult male ghost is Danny. He, too, worked for the theater but, unlike Fritz, did not die in the building. Sadly, Danny was a drug addict who succumbed to his addiction when he was about 30. Since both Danny and Fritz have indicated that they are happy to spend their ever-after at the Vogue, the owners have decided that the ghosts shall be left to haunt in peace.

And so, to the casual passersby on the sidewalk who are unaware of the theater's past, the Vogue today might seem like just another dark theater. It most certainly is not.

Spirits of the Palace

The Palace Theater, on Vine Street in the heart of Hollywood, opened in 1927 as the Hollywood Playhouse. Over the years, the three-story building has been used as a venue for a variety of entertainment forms, including rock 'n' roll shows, radio shows and television shows as well as for more traditional theatrical fare such as stage plays. If you think that such a long and varied history might have left the place haunted, you'd be quite right. The Palace is *very* haunted.

One of the most intriguing ghosts is that of a man wearing a tuxedo. Witnesses always puzzle over the fact that when the formally attired man appears—usually on the stage—his face is transparent and he appears not to have any feet. Historical research into various incarnations of the building over the years finally resolved this enigma. It was discovered that the stage area has been raised since the time of the man's death. The ghost's feet are certainly still attached—they are simply no longer visible to mortals because the phantom is walking on the floor level that existed when he was still alive, a level some 6" below the currently visible one. While that simple mechanical alteration accounts for the ghost's apparent lack of feet, the riddle of why he has no facial features remains unanswered.

Another set of phantom activities around the theater involved the sounds of jazz piano music coming from an empty, locked room. Although a piano was stored in that room, the door was locked and, when it was unlocked to see who was making the music, no signs of the mysterious musician could be found.

Ghosts are often associated with randomly occurring pockets of cold air, and the Palace has more than its share of those. Some of the cool areas may be caused by the ghost in the tuxedo, but at other times the temperature anomalies are associated with a scent of perfume, indicating that there is at least one other resident spirit haunting the place, most likely a female.

People who work in haunted buildings often report that they hear their names being called by a disembodied voice. One specter at the Palace employs a slightly different approach. He doesn't call out; his style is much more "up close and personal." He or she taps unsuspecting people on the shoulder with an invisible hand. It's quite an effective and unnerving attention-grabber.

During the early 1990s, a security guard brought in a large dog to keep him company during an overnight shift at the theater. For a while all was quiet, but around 2:30 AM, for no reason that the guard could see, the dog pricked up his ears and began to stare intently at a corner of the stage. When the guard unleashed the dog, the animal ran to the spot he'd been watching. Seconds before the dog reached the corner of the stage, the guard noticed a section of the left-hand side curtain move. There, the guard clearly saw the now-familiar—but still odd—formally dressed, faceless and footless apparition. Seconds later, the image disappeared.

While all of these phantoms seem to be permanent residents, there are other ghosts in the building who are only seen occasionally. When they are spotted, it's always up on the balcony. These specters are an elderly couple in 1930s-style clothes and they may or may not be responsible for some or all of the ghostly conversations that have been heard coming from that area when it's known to have been completely empty—of warm-blooded folk, anyway.

It would seem that the ghosts at the Palace do their part to keep the area near the famous intersection of Hollywood and Vine as interesting as possible.

Sam Warner's Specter

The story of Sam Warner haunting the old Warner Pacific Theater on Hollywood Boulevard is, in many ways, an absolutely classic Hollywood ghost story.

In the late 1920s, Harry, Albert, Sam and Jack Warner invested everything they had in the creation of Warner Brothers Studio. They worked hard, took enormous risks and experienced at least as many failures as they did successes. This amount of emotional investment is bound to have an effect on any environment.

The brothers became totally committed to a radically new concept in movies—the talkies. This was not only an expensive experiment, but also a daring one. Sound in film was an idea that many people were sure would never catch on. Why, those skeptics reasoned, would audiences want to hear actors talking? The movies were what they were—an art form that consisted of actors pantomiming their roles—nothing more, nothing less.

Those preconceived notions were about to be changed and, in large part, it was Warner Brothers Studios that would bring about the shift when they released a musical called *The Jazz Singer*. In order to reap as much of a financial reward from their investment as possible, the brothers were, at the same time, building a spectacular new movie house. They hoped to simultaneously release their benchmark flick and open their landmark theater.

To accomplish all of this, the brothers Warner needed to divide the responsibilities of the workload. Sam Warner held himself accountable for the construction of the theater. Despite his best efforts, however, the building was not ready in time to host the first-ever run of their amazing and daring technological accomplishment. Sam was utterly devastated. He had pushed himself to exhaustion, but still failed in his mission. In October of 1927, at the age of 40, Sam Warner died of a cerebral hemorrhage. Later that week, *The Jazz Singer* opened in New York to wild acclaim, but without any of the brothers Warner present. The theater to which Sam had devoted so much of himself opened the following spring.

For many years after his death, Sam Warner continued to prove his sense of determination where that theater was concerned. Security workers around the building have said that they are sure it is Sam who is haunting the place to this day. The fact that his image has frequently been seen, and recognized, confirms those convictions. Even passers by on the street have witnessed his ghostly image in the lobby of the theater.

In the early 1970s, workers watched in rapt fascination as the theater's resident entity calmly walked through the open door of the elevator before pushing the button to close the doors. Seconds later these same people listened to the familiar sound of the lift ascending.

Although he's not often seen any more, Sam Warner could still be heard moving about in parts of the building that were known to be empty until quite recently. Today, the man's once restless spirit may be calmed because the building he worked so hard to complete has recently been renovated to become the Hollywood Entertainment Museum.

With this honor, one hopes that Sam's soul will finally be able to rest.

Barbara Smith has always been a collector of folklore and in recent years has successfully combined this interest with her other passion—writing. Her best-selling Ghost Stories series has resulted in an overwhelming response from readers who in turn have wanted to share their paranormal experiences.

Be sure to enjoy these other spine-tingling Ghost Stories books by Barbara Smith:

Ghost Stories of California
1-55105-237-7 • 5.25" x 8.25"
• 224 pp. • $10.95

Ghost Stories of Washington
1-55105-260-1 • 5.25" x 8.25"
• 232 pp. • $10.95

Ghost Stories of the Rocky Mountains
1-55105-165-6 • 5.25" x 8.25"
• 240 pp. • $10.95

Ontario Ghost Stories
1-55105-203-2 • 5.25" x 8.25"
• 240 pp. • $10.95

Ghost Stories of Manitoba
1-55105-180-X • 5.25" x 8.25"• 240 pp. • $10.95
1998 National Bestseller

Ghost Stories and Mysterious Creatures of British Columbia
1-55105-172-9 • 5.25" x 8.25" • 240 pp. • $10.95

More Ghost Stories of Alberta
1-55105-083-8 • 5.25" x 8.25" • 232 pp. • $10.95
1996 National Bestseller

and by Jo-Anne Christensen:

Ghost Stories of Illinois
1-55105-239-3 • 5.25" x 8.25" • 240 pp. • $10.95

More Ghost Stories of Saskatchewan
1-55105-276-8 • 5.25" x 8.25" • 200 pp. • $10.95

Available at your local bookseller or from Lone Pine Publishing
US: 1-800-518-3541 • Fax 1-800-548-1169
Canada: 1-800-661-9017 • Fax 1-800-424-7173